MOTHERING ON OUR OWN

Published in 2025 by Hardie Grant Books, an imprint of Hardie Grant Publishing

Hardie Grant Books (Melbourne)
Wurundjeri Country
Level 11, 36 Wellington Street
Collingwood, Victoria 3066

Hardie Grant North America
2912 Telegraph Ave
Berkeley, California 94705
hardiegrant.com/books

Hardie Grant acknowledges the Traditional Owners of the Country on which we work, the Wurundjeri People of the Kulin Nation and the Gadigal People of the Eora Nation, and recognises their continuing connection to the land, waters and culture. We pay our respects to their Elders past and present.

All rights reserved. No part of this publication may be reproduced, stored in a retrieval system or transmitted in any form by any means, electronic, mechanical, photocopying, recording or otherwise, without the prior written permission of the publishers and copyright holders.

The moral rights of the authors have been asserted.

Introduction and selection © Rachel Maksimovic 2025
Individual stories © retained by the authors, who assert their rights to be known as the author of their work.

 A catalogue record for this book is available from the National Library of Australia

Mothering on Our Own
ISBN 978 1 76145 125 6
ISBN 978 1 76144 346 6 (ebook)

10 9 8 7 6 5 4 3 2 1

Publisher: Tahlia Anderson
Head of Editorial: Jasmin Chua
Project Editor: Lauren Carta
Editor: Emma Driver
Creative Director: Kristin Thomas
Designer: Alissa Dinallo
Typesetter: Hannah Schubert
Head of Production: Todd Rechner
Production Controller: Jessica Harvie

Cover image and author photograph by Emily-Rose Simmons

Printed in Australia by Griffin Press, an Accredited ISO AS/NZS 14001 Environmental Management System printer.

 The paper this book is printed on is certified against the Forest Stewardship Council® Standards. Griffin Press holds FSC® chain of custody certification SCS-COC-001185. FSC® promotes environmentally responsible, socially beneficial and economically viable management of the world's forests.

MOTHERING ON OUR OWN

30 stories of love, hope &
navigating single motherhood

Edited by RACHEL MAKSIMOVIC

Hardie Grant
BOOKS

CONTENTS

RACHEL MAKSIMOVIC
Introduction vi

RACHEL MAKSIMOVIC
On going it alone 8

MAGGIE KELLY
On green sprouts 16

ELLIDY PULLIN
On growing around grief 26

JESSICA DOVER
On forgiveness 38

MARCIA LEONE
On finding the rainbow after the rain 48

NATASHA ROFE
On embracing life after loss 54

MONTANA LOWER
On finding a village 60

RENEE STASKA
On mothering through adversity 64

ABBY GILMORE
On a new family bond 70

JACINTHA FIELD
On becoming your own hero 76

ELIZABETH ANILE
On making lemonade 86

AMIE ROHAN
On holding on to hope 92

ELLIE LEMONS
On redefining co-parenting 98

KELLIE MOSES
On healing your soul 102

EMILY MCKAY
On the hardest decisions 108

ZOE GEORGE
On finding your confidence 112

GRETA BRIDGETTE
On life on the other side 118

ANONYMOUS
On surviving with strength 124

HIND AL-AZZAM
On becoming a teen mum 132

MICHELLE RYAN
On choosing happiness 138

EMMA JUNE
On acceptance fatigue 144

ANNA SQUELCH
On choosing motherhood first 150

CARLI POPPLEWELL
On embracing new realities 156

MELISSA MAI
On reconnecting with your heart 166

ANONYMOUS
On leaving domestic violence 172

OLA NECHYPORENKO
On the long road to peace 178

AMY CRELLIN
On beautiful chaos 188

SAMANTHA APPEL
On dreams and determination 194

LEAH PATARA
On creating safe havens 200

EVIE FARRELL
On the road less travelled 206

Resources 212
Acknowledgements 216

RACHEL MAKSIMOVIC
Introduction

I was twenty-eight years old and had been living abroad in Indonesia for around six months when I fell pregnant. My circumstances were unusual and less than ideal. I was in a new relationship with someone whose cultural background was significantly different to mine. Even though I held out some hope we could work things out, I think I knew deep down that keeping the baby would mean I would end up a solo mum. My gut told me, for whatever reason, that this was meant to be my journey.

When I was twenty weeks pregnant, I became a solo mum. I vividly recall organising a meeting with my partner's non-English-speaking family and arranging for an interpreter to help me express my needs and desires. At that moment, surrounded by unfamiliar faces in a foreign country, the weight of my situation hit me. I returned to Australia and, despite hopes of maintaining a connection with my baby's father, I soon realised that I would be raising our child alone.

INTRODUCTION

I had always been a very relaxed and carefree girl. However, during my pregnancy I felt the weight of anxiety, and was flooded with feelings of depression and darkness. Since that time I have tried to pinpoint those feelings. I think not knowing what was to come frightened me – all the unknowns. How was I going to do things? How was it going to look? How would my life end up? I was so confused about what was happening to me that I experienced panic attacks for the first time in my life. They would always come on late at night when I was sitting on the couch. I would be overwhelmed with breathlessness, and I would go into a spiral. *I have completely fucked up my life* is where it always landed.

I started to read books and autobiographies. No successful person had ever become great without having challenges in their lives, so maybe this would be mine. Then I started to research famous single mums. There were so many of them. My sister told me about Janine Allis, founder of Boost Juice, who was a single mum before going on to create a hugely successful business and remarry. I found Pip Edwards, who raised her son as a solo mother and went on to create a cult Australian fashion brand. There was Terri Irwin, who devastatingly lost the love of her life and had to grieve for him while raising two children and continuing to manage Steve's legacy. I was so inspired reading about these women. *Well, if they could do it*, I thought, *why can't I?*

—

My son, Lenny, was four months old when I realised there wasn't enough support for solo mothers. The online space was evolving, with new resources, pages and groups to help support and educate parents, but they were all missing many of the unique challenges related to single motherhood, which made me feel even more isolated and invisible. Like all mothers, I struggled with so many aspects of the early days – sleep, breastfeeding, taking time for myself (even though that never happened) – but what surprised me the most was how alone I felt. It felt like no one could even begin to understand what I was going through. I had no idea what I would go on to create but the feelings began to stir inside of me.

I bought an A3 piece of paper, like the ones I'd used at school, and created a mind map. First I wrote SINGLE MUM in huge capital letters in the middle of the page. Around that I started to list issues that felt connected to single motherhood: loneliness and isolation, finances, not getting time to yourself, managing a career, co-parenting, the Family Court process and dating.

The poster sat in my lounge room for more than a year. It even moved to different houses with me as I moved around the place trying to find my feet. It remained a constant in my life, sitting at the forefront of my mind and my lounge room, because this journey of single motherhood was so great and so big that it deserved to be put in the spotlight. Over those years I would go through moments of feeling completely empowered, and ready to take on a project that would help support women who were navigating single and solo motherhood. And then I would fall into times and circumstances where I felt completely debilitated by the very challenges that were written up on that poster on my wall. How could I help others when I too was constantly falling to my knees?

INTRODUCTION

I write a bit more about my own struggle in the next chapter. In particular, there was a time when I felt like I had well and truly hit rock bottom. I am not sure what happened after that point, but things started to shift in my life. Lenny had turned four, and the demands of a toddler felt like a distant memory. Somehow my body and my mind were forgetting what those years of sleep deprivation were like. I felt ready to open up my heart again and date; I had more time and capacity to work; and I got an au pair, which gave me snippets of freedom that I hadn't thought I'd experience for many years to come. I started to feel like I could dream again, and all of my aspirations suddenly felt a little closer.

I once heard someone describe a community as an emergency room, with a triage system to prioritise those in urgent need. At the time, I related to this deeply, feeling like I was the one in need of immediate care. A community, much like a hospital, supports and attends first to those who walk through the doors and need the most urgent care. After navigating the challenges of solo motherhood for five years, I began to understand the analogy in a new light. I no longer felt the same urgency for attention; instead, I had grown enough to open those doors for others, offering support in return.

It started with a podcast. I had no idea what I was doing but I knew I needed somewhere to have these conversations, to put single and solo motherhood in the spotlight. It would be for women who felt just like I had – isolated and invisible, trying to feel seen and heard in their experiences. Better yet, it would help them discover new ways to navigate through these periods through shared stories, resources and new tools.

I started *Mothering on My Own* with a girlfriend of mine, Jessica Dover (who features in this book). We were childhood friends and had stayed in touch while living in different states over the years. When Jess announced her separation online, I reached out and we found ourselves connected once again. The response when we launched the podcast was overwhelming, and the messages continue to flood into our inbox. Listeners often share the feeling of drowning in their experiences, and say the podcast has given them hope. As her business grew and needed more of her time, Jess was no longer able to do the podcast with me, but we are both so proud of what we started together.

Surprisingly, *Mothering on My Own* has offered me so much too. Motherhood is a journey of love, resilience, and sacrifice – and for single and solo mothers, it can often feel like an uncharted path, one walked with few guides and even fewer words of solidarity. I spent many years feeling like I was the only person in the world, but now I feel connected – I feel community.

The journey I've taken with the podcast has been cathartic and healing in many ways. I am constantly in awe of the women I speak to and who share their stories with me, whether it's on the podcast, in these very pages or in my DMs. I am constantly in awe of the strength and resilience of the women who continue to show up for their children every day. As I watch women in my Facebook group creating their own local groups to catch up and connect, I feel so grateful that I get to play a small part in helping them build support networks.

—

The journey of single motherhood is one that can be marked by many challenges: loneliness, financial strain, exhaustion, abuse, co-parenting, blending families, dating, and sometimes the burden of judgement from a society that often fails to recognise the fullness of the lives of solo mothers. Too often, their voices go unheard. This book exists to change that. Each of these thirty stories is a testament to the incredible courage and tenacity these women show every day. They are the backbone of their families. This book amplifies their stories, not only to celebrate their strength but to validate their struggles, and to remind them – and all of us – that they are not alone. In the wisdom they share, you will find both comfort and hope.

To the women who have nervously picked up this book, still in the throes of an unhappy relationship and unsure how they could possibly survive single motherhood – I hope this book gives you hope.

To the women who are in the trenches of single motherhood, feeling debilitated by the challenges that come with the journey – I hope this book gives you peace.

To the single and solo mothers reading these pages who feel alone and isolated in their experience – I hope this book helps you to find strength and solidarity, no matter how overwhelming the journey may seem.

MOTHERING ON OUR OWN

RACHEL MAKSIMOVIC
On going it alone

In 2018, I left my full-time job to start my own business in digital marketing. My dream was to live life on my own terms, with the freedom to do what I wanted, when I wanted and wherever I wanted. Within just two months, I had matched my previous income. With this newfound freedom, my first instinct was to relocate to Bali – a place brimming with entrepreneurs, dreamers, and those in search of their own 'eat, pray, love' experience. Little did I know mine would become 'eat, pray, pregnant'.

Like many, I felt a longing to discover something more meaningful in my life. Despite the common advice to find joy and happiness wherever you are, I found myself still searching for something elusive. This quest for fulfilment stemmed partly from a painful dating experience in my early twenties, which led me to close myself off from relationships and intimacy for much of that decade. My journey to Bali was an attempt to break free from that pattern.

On 29 June 2018, I unexpectedly met the man who would become the father of my child. It was my birthday, and I decided to book a surf lesson with a popular surf instructor in Canggu, hoping to start the day off on a positive note. I had only been living overseas for just over a month and was feeling a bit lonely. Little did I know that simple decision would alter the course of my life.

Five months later, I found out I was pregnant, and soon after that I realised I would be raising my son alone. Unlike usual pregnancy announcements, with mine there was no screaming or hooting or hugging or big congratulations. I understood it at the time, of course – I wasn't even sure *I* was excited. But my circumstances were unusual and everyone around me feared what this meant for my future. So did I.

I was supported, but it became very clear early on that the journey was going to be a lonely one. Shopping for baby clothes, having ultrasounds and planning for life with a newborn was all done in isolation. At one of my check-ups, my doctor did a mental health check and I came up significantly high on their chart for predicting postnatal depression. *Great!* I thought. *Even they think I'm fucked.*

I was excited for this little boy to enter my life. However, the fear of the unknown continued to bog me down, and I spent most of my pregnancy ebbing and flowing between states of total despair and excitement.

I grew up with very few single mothers around me. I was still very much influenced by how society saw them, and I feared that becoming a solo mother would mean I would never have any money, never be able to travel, never have the career that I dreamed of, and never have another partner or any other children. I thought I would be looked down upon in this world.

I remember that around thirty weeks into my pregnancy I called my mum and made a declaration to her. I was sitting on the end of my bed, overwhelmed with tears. *This is it for me*, I told her. I was still shit-bloody-scared, but from that day onwards, I was no longer going to let the debilitating fear stop me from creating whatever the hell I wanted from this new life trajectory. I know how easily I can sit in fear and misery, and I realised it was this mindset – the one that said my life was over – that could break me. I decided I was never going to let that happen.

I decided that I was going to rewrite the script of my own journey of solo motherhood. It would be a blank canvas, and I was going to create my own new version, full of financial abundance, travel, friendships, a full and exciting career in something I love, new experiences, and a forever love who would take on my child as his own and grow our family. While many of these still aren't my reality, I have held on to this faith throughout the years and still believe with every fibre of my being it will come.

What if this little boy, and this life that I have been thrust into, were exactly what I needed to create something even better than I could have created before?

I had a magical birth bringing Lenny into the world. I actually have a video of my childbirth, and you can hear me repeating, 'Oh my god oh my god oh my god,' on rotation for about two minutes. I was in complete and total shock. But my favourite part of that video is at the end when I said, 'Oh my god – I fucking did it!' I feel like it represents so much of my journey over the last five years.

I could probably write a whole book on the challenges that I have faced over the last five years. Many have taken me to the depths of a darkness I couldn't even begin to comprehend. The one thing that remained constant over those years was the commitment that I made to myself that day, sitting on the end of my bed. One foot in front of the other, step by step, challenge by challenge – I was determined I would find my way through them all. I used the women who had gone before me as guideposts, reminders of what was possible.

From there, my journey of solo motherhood proved to be both magical and arduous. The early months were filled with moments of exhaustion and overwhelming responsibility as I navigated the challenges of parenting without any support. The relentless demands of caring for a newborn left little time for respite, and the isolation weighed heavily on me.

I was lucky enough to grow up in the same family home until my twenties, which has only highlighted the stark difference between my son's childhood and my own. In the first three years of Lenny's life we had moved homes eight times and lived in three different cities.

There are a multitude of reasons for the moves – owners selling their home that I'd been renting, and now had to vacate; a scary neighbour who harassed me daily, which involved police reports and an urgent relocation for our safety. On reflection, I also feel like part of the moving was an underlying seeking of a place that felt like home, a place that could somehow solve all of my life's problems – which it never did. Learning to find home within myself was something I would later need to discover.

For a while, I adored living in the Northern Rivers, as it much more suits the lifestyle I love to live. But as a solo mum, it also felt a little too isolating and, once again, I felt I needed to make a change. I had connected with a mutual friend who offered me their caravan in Melbourne for six months, and I jumped at the opportunity. I sold my car to buy a four-wheel drive and left behind my rental to begin this new adventure. An hour into my drive back to Melbourne, I found out that the caravan I had been planning to live in for the next six months was no longer available for me to use. I felt my world crumble underneath me. We were on our way to Melbourne, but now I had no idea what we were going to do.

There came a moment when the sheer weight of relentless financial, physical and emotional demands became too much to bear. Despite months of searching, I couldn't secure a rental property in Victoria. As a less-than-ideal tenant and unable to purchase a property, I felt utterly alone, and terrified for myself and my son. Where on earth would we go?

After spending days in a hotel (at $300 a night) and depleting the little savings I had, I reached my breaking point. I remember the moment so clearly. I was driving around Melbourne and for the first time in years, I had no creative ideas or solutions. I was petrified and in tears. I genuinely had no idea where we were going to sleep that night.

Of course, I had people around me who wouldn't let us sleep on the streets, but I was exhausted. Exhausted from asking for help, and from feeling like I had to rely on others to carry the heavy load for us. A shared living space with a toddler and a dog is no easy situation either. Most of my family live in Adelaide, but I knew Melbourne was the place for me; I felt that if I left and went back to Adelaide, I would get trapped there. It wasn't an option.

Swallowing my pride was excruciating, but I knew I had to do it. It was the first time that I actually admitted, 'I need help.' I found myself at a women's crisis centre, unsure of what assistance they could offer but acutely aware that I had nowhere else to turn. This moment marked a significant turning point in my journey. It was a humbling moment I won't ever forget.

For four years, I had shouldered the weight of being a solo mother alone, and I had never fully acknowledged the extent of my struggles. It was almost cathartic to finally relinquish my defences and embrace the support I so desperately needed. From that moment on, something deep shifted in me and a fire was lit under me that has brought me to the life I lead today. Due to the housing crisis, I ended up spending eight weeks in a hotel room, arranged by the crisis centre, at a rate I could afford. While that time was not easy, I felt so grateful for the support and the safety of that room.

When Lenny and I drove past the hotel recently, he mentioned that he missed living there. While my memories aren't as fond, I do remember using this time to fill up our lives with gratitude. It was in this hotel room that we began our nightly routine of sharing our gratitudes for the day, which we still share with each other every night. At the time he would talk about his babycinos and the things we had done together. I would share my gratitude for having a roof over our heads, the safety of a place to call a temporary home, the fact that we were able to have our dog with us. It fills my heart to know that Lenny looks at our time in the hotel as beautiful and happy – something I worked so hard to create.

When I reflect on the beginning of this journey, I often wish I could go back to my pregnant self – the one who was so petrified about what life was about to become – and give her the biggest bear hug.

I'd tell her that not only would everything be okay, but it would be better than okay.

I'd tell her that the love she would feel for this little boy would be bigger and stronger than anything she could imagine.

I'd tell her that, yes, there would be challenges, some really big ones too, but not to worry – because she would overcome them, just as she always had.

I'd tell her that, with time, both she and her son would build a relationship with his dad, one filled with love, respect and understanding.

I'd tell her that there would be a heartbreak and even though it will hurt like hell, it will show her that another love was possible at the right time, with the right person.

I'd tell her that the things you want might not come quickly, but keep faith and lean into the process, it's never failed you.

I'd tell her that it's okay if you don't have a spare minute to invest in dating – that time will come and your relationship with your son will feel better for it.

I'd tell her that building support and community takes work and many times along this journey you will feel lonely, but there will be magical people that show up for you from where you least expect it.

I'd tell her that she would grow to let go of the resentment she felt towards having a family that didn't look 'traditional'. Instead, she'd come to revel in the beautifully chaotic home they built together – filled with love, laughter, and her two German Shepherds.

I'd tell her that life would be filled with so much joy, so much goodness, and more magic than she ever thought possible.

And that there is so much more to come.

MAGGIE KELLY
On green sprouts

Single motherhood, month #1

Before I moved from Brisbane to Melbourne, the split had been fine. Not 'fine' in the way of a late bus, or a broken watch, or a forgotten umbrella. It was 'fine' in the sense that as far as catastrophic life experiences go, I was still standing. I had only been married five months before my husband and I decided to separate. We were in our mid-thirties and had a two-year-old daughter, Minty. It wasn't great, but I had felt oddly calm about the whole thing. After years of sitting with an oily feeling of discomfort, cornered into a life that I didn't feel was really mine, I was finally on my own.

All around me, friends and family lingered, waiting for the moment when I would crumble. But I didn't. My ex-husband and I had made the decision together and were both optimistic that we would be far better as co-parents than as a couple. Our existing move to Melbourne would still go ahead, albeit separately, and I was buoyed with an airy optimism that I would soon be back in the city I loved. Boxes were packed, and the flotsam and jetsam of five years together was neatly divided: you take that lamp, I'll take this picture, we'll split the towels. It was, well, *fine*.

But almost immediately after arriving, it wasn't fine. Not at all.

The day I arrived in Melbourne was icy. As the taxi pulled up to my new apartment block, a barefaced and staunch brick stack, my heart fell. It was miserable. Melbourne was transitioning into winter, and it looked as though a tin of grey paint had been spilled across the city, the technicolour world of tropical Queensland far, far away. What would usually have been a leafy green street in East Melbourne was barren, with spindly branches scratching against the wind and a silvery sky turning dark by early afternoon. The adrenaline had worn off, and I was left to consider the harsh new reality that I had stepped into. I was here, in this ugly brick apartment, on my own. I was a *single mother*. I could barely say the words out loud.

What had been a picture-perfect separation turned into hell overnight. In the first week of shared custody, when Minty left me for the first time she screamed for me for so long that I could hear her calling, 'Mummy! Mummy!' from blocks away. I howled, my back against the front door, clutching her teddy bear and feeling like a limb had been hacked off. My ex-husband, until then promising friendship and support, went dark. Communication was severed. After being surrounded by friends and family in Queensland for years, I was suddenly and irrevocably alone in Melbourne.

In the space of a few weeks, I dropped two dress sizes. I barely slept, and my under-eyes took on the colour of deep purple bruises, hollowing out my face. I was mothering like a robot, barely managing to do the minimum: cook, feed, clean. I lay awake most nights, staring at the ceiling of the tiny apartment and wondering what the point of living was. I wouldn't know it yet, but I was slipping into a deep pit of clinical depression. By the end of the year, I would be on two different types of antidepressants, plus a sleeping tablet.

The early days were the worst. Cold winter mornings made getting out the door almost too much to bear. I would drink two huge cups of black coffee before bundling Minty in a solid layer of beanies, mittens, jackets and blankets and heading out to daycare. Down four flights of stairs we would go, Minty's arms tight around my neck. I would walk down this set of stairs hundreds of times and still, every time, I imagined myself tripping, falling, dropping Minty, crushing her. The fear never went away.

On my second day in the apartment, I found a note pinned to our pram: *Continue to leave this pram in the shared area and I will throw it in the bin.* For a few weeks I lugged the pram up and down the four flights of stairs, Minty on one hip, bags digging into my arm. In the end, I wrote to the landlord, explaining I was on my own and couldn't carry it. Please, I asked, please let me store it downstairs, resenting myself as I typed those five horrible words: *I am a single mother.*

Rain, hail or shine, Minty and I would trudge back and forth to daycare. As we passed the convenience store with the oversized ice cream on the sign, she would repeat the same request over and over to the point of madness: ice cream, ice cream, ice cream, ice cream. I would imagine pushing the pram onto the road and walking away. I wanted to hide from the world but had no choice but to air my filthy grief in public – I didn't have a car, not even a driver's licence. It had been nothing more than a quirk until then, a funny Maggie-ism that amused people. 'You don't drive?' people would ask in mock-horror, and I'd give a coy smirk. Silly Maggie. Cute Maggie. Now it was a lack that haunted me every day.

Before then, see, I'd had a partner to patch up my holes, the ying to my yang. I couldn't drive, but he was terrible with taxes. I couldn't change a light bulb, but he was handy at fixing everything. He was my husband. My partner. A man who would drive us around in our family car, listening to classical music on long drives. He cleaned the windscreen at the service stations and installed the baby seat when I was heavily pregnant. My man who used to keep salt-and-vinegar chips in the glove box to help my motion sickness. I thought about my hand on his knee as he drove, squeezing it three times. I. Love. You.

Eventually, Minty and I would arrive at daycare, a concrete block with reflective windows that sat on a four-lane main road in Melbourne's north. It was ugly, and even to this day it gives me a knot of anxiety when I pass it. I hated those early morning drop-offs: I can still feel the stare of morning commuters, dead-eyed, waiting for us to cross the road, holding them up, in the way. *Hurry up.* Minty would cling to me, hysterical, wailing when the daycare workers tried to peel her off. *Hurry up.* I'd look down and make a beeline for the door. Down the stairs, avoiding eye contact with the other parents. A door, another door. I'm out on the street, morning traffic blazing past me. My eyes stinging with tears. *Just hurry up!*

Most days I would get home and just cry. I was bone tired. Tired of being sad, tired of being tired. Life felt like an exercise in discovering new ways of failing. Everyone else seemed to be building happy lives while mine burned away, the smouldering remains of something wonderful. I was a shadow, black smoke, that moved through the world in constant pain.

Within a few months of arriving in Melbourne, I lost my job. I thought I was doing well at hiding my pain, but I wasn't. I lost interest in everything. As I recalibrated to this new financial reality, debt started to pile up like little piles of rubble, innocuous at the start but slowly forming an insurmountable mountain. For the first time in my life, I was poor, properly poor, and eased the pain by creating lists in my phone of all things I'd buy when things were better:

- New running shoes
- Botox
- Underwear (everyday)
- Underwear (fancy)
- Get my hair done
- Bike for Minty
- A car
- New frying pan

A few weeks later I found a new job, and during the day I would sit at my desk for hours on end, working, the apartment air thick with silence. Occasionally I would have a video call with a client, slipping on a smile for forty minutes before quietly removing it once we had hung up. As the sun began to set, I'd go to collect Minty. We'd walk home in silence, watching black ravens picking rubbish out of roadside bins.

After her bath, I would watch Minty eat chicken nuggets with tomato sauce in front of *Bluey*, slick and sweet in her flannelette pyjamas, robe and slippers. She seemed happier, despite it all. She started to make jokes and chattered away about friends from daycare. As she blossomed in the world, I could not help but feel I was doing the opposite: a flower slowly shrivelling, dropping, decaying into the earth as if I had never been there in the first place.

Single motherhood, month #17

Today I felt the first warm wind of spring and my heart swelled, nostalgic for something I can't quite identify. Our new apartment is a block from the ocean and this morning I could smell the salty, sinewy smell of the seaweed that laces Elwood Beach. For the millionth time, I think about how profoundly lucky we are to be near the stretch of bay, with sun and salt water on tap whenever needed. Moving here was the first time I had listened to a gut feeling, maybe ever, and we are revelling in its rewards.

 The sun pours through the big kitchen windows, and I move around quietly, waking up the house for the day ahead. Minty snores from my bedroom and I poke my head in to check she's okay. I notice the indoor plant in the corner of the room unfurling a fresh green leaf. There's new life in the air.

 I tiptoe into the kitchen to fresh coffee on the stovetop, the pot burbling to tell me it's ready. We have carved out routines that bookend our days as a family of two, with morning and evening rituals carved deeply like love-heart initials in a backyard tree. Coffee, green juice, shower. Hair, make-up, wake up Minty. Dress her, dress me, feed the cats. Heat up her toastie. Sing to the radio. Pack my bag for work. Lock up and leave. Our new place is at ground level, no stairs, and I inhale deeply as we step outside onto the quiet seaside street. It's a good day.

'The sun is following us,' says Minty, pointing to the twinkling light spilling through the elms. 'Yes, baby,' I reply, 'it follows us wherever we go. Wherever we are in the world.' I watch her think about that as she takes another bite of her toasted cheese-and-ham sandwich, cogs turning in her little mind.

We walk slowly through the local park, past ponds and misty stretches of field, ducks flapping as they skim around the marshland. Minty's new daycare is nestled into a quiet suburban street. It's reminiscent of another era: an old Victorian home converted into a childcare, creaky and wooden and lovely. It smells of toast and the sweet milkiness of babies. I push on the low wooden gate, the white paint worn off its handle, smoothed right down to the wood. A million hands having pushed it open and closed over the years. It makes me feel happy when I see that gate, like I'm part of something without even trying. Minty squats by the herb garden at the entry and points to a mint leaf. 'Minty!' she says, pointing. She's so clever.

On the bus into the office, I make a mental note to get cash out for Maria, my driving instructor. She comes up to my armpit, a Russian babushka who smacks my arm if I do something wrong and smokes slim cigarettes that she holds in her purple fingernails. She is exhausting, and wonderful, and one of my favourite people I have been blessed with over the last year. She is teaching me to reverse park and to turn corners slowly – and a few other important life lessons along the way.

'You need to stop looking for excuses,' she tells me in a thick Russian accent. 'You need to start looking for solutions.'

My days are a happy blur of people and meetings and writing. After months of expending energy I didn't have on jobs that didn't care, I gave myself the grace of taking something less intense – not easy, but not overly challenging either. It's a big, safe ship of a company, with plenty of budget and new offices and room to breathe. It's not a job I would have ever wished for myself, but it has given me the mental and physical space to rest and carve back some time to just live. Here, folks eat together in the communal lunch hall, the adult version of the bustling American high-school cafeterias I used to dream about as a teenager. It has oddly become one of the happiest jobs I've ever taken. My life, suddenly slow, is happy. I am happy.

Of course, happiness is delicate. I am deeply proud of what I have built, but if I let myself, I fall backwards into the same hole I have only just crawled out of. I look around, as if suddenly sober at a party, and hate everything. I hate my crumbling Art Deco beachside shack. I hate my middle-management, normal-person job. I am still poor, I am still sad, I am still single. I will live out my days alone, without a man to drive my child to daycare or install baby seats or keep salt-and-vinegar chips in the glove box. I am unlovable; I am a *single mother*.

The trick here is not to believe the narrative. As you drink up the many stories of survival in this book, you will see that from the very moment you become a single mother – be it from trauma or joy – you are getting stronger. You are fighting millennia of patriarchal priming, a lifetime of education both anecdotal and actual that tells you that parenthood is done as a dyad. To do it alone feels alien because we're taught it is alien. And, like most things in this world, you must commit yourself to unlearning these teachings in order to be truly happy.

Seventeen months has placed me a universe away from where I was at the start of my journey. The world, like that oddly resilient pot plant in my room, continues to unfurl new green leaves. I have dated several men in varying states of commitment. I have set up an entire house. I have made a new friend, another single mother who lives a few streets over and has quickly become the heartbeat of my new life. I have single-handedly dragged myself out of a thick black swamp of depression, and never once crumbled. This is magic. This is *single mother* magic.

Seventeen months ago, the words 'single mother' cut like a knife; today I wear the title as a badge of honour. I wonder where I will be a year from now. How exciting it is to finally be excited. And for anyone reading this, whatever stage of your single mother journey you are in, let this be a lighthouse in the fog: you won't just be 'fine'. You'll be *great*.

ELLIDY PULLIN
On growing around grief

Chumpy and I had crossed paths a few times, running in similar friendship circles, but it wasn't until a friend's twenty-first birthday party that our lives truly collided. Across the dance floor our eyes locked, and we were drawn to each other. We met in the middle, and with our first kiss our love story began.

Life with Chumpy felt effortless. Despite his frequent travels as a professional athlete, we found ways to stay connected, growing closer even while we spent time apart. We came from different worlds but fit together perfectly. Chumpy was grounded, determined and kind – qualities that made me fall in love with him more each day.

Wednesday 8 July 2020 started like any other day. I woke up in our house on the Gold Coast to see Chumpy standing at the window, looking out at the still ocean. It was a calm, beautiful morning, and he was preparing to go spearfishing – a hobby he was deeply passionate about. He loved the ocean, and spearfishing had become one of his biggest joys. He often brought home fresh fish for dinner.

I stayed in bed a little longer as he got ready. We had friends visiting for dinner that evening, so he planned to dive for our dinner in the morning while I took our dog, Rummi, for a beach walk. We agreed to meet later for brunch at one of our favourite cafes.

As he drove out of the garage, I stood there wondering if he'd shut the garage door. Sensing my frustration, he got out of the car, teased me for being dramatic and pulled me into a big hug. That hug is a moment I replay in my mind over and over, wishing I could hold on to him forever.

Later, after my walk, my mum arrived to help clean the house. A neighbour knocked on the door, mentioning a Facebook post about a man being pulled from the water at Palm Beach. At first, I didn't think much of it, but then a wave of panic hit me: *What if it's Chumpy?*

I yelled for Mum, and we rushed to the beach. When we arrived, the scene was chaotic – paramedics, police and a crowd had gathered. I couldn't bring myself to look closely at the commotion, still convinced that even if it was Chumpy, he would be fine. Maybe he was hurt, but he'd be okay.

I approached a police officer who was sitting alone and told him my partner had gone spearfishing that morning. He asked if Chumpy had any tattoos. When I described them, his silence told me everything I needed to know.

Time blurred after that. Mum and I were taken to the surf club, where the police asked me a series of questions. I avoided asking too many myself, as if not knowing would make it less real. It wasn't until they called his parents and I heard the words spoken out loud that I began to grasp the devastating truth. *Chumpy's dead.* I hate saying it. I fucking hate the word. *He's gone.*

—

In the days after Chumpy's death, I clung to the hope that I might already be pregnant. We had been trying for a baby, even discussing IVF.

In Queensland, where I live, you have up to thirty-six hours to retrieve sperm from a deceased person's body. It was a process I had never heard of.

The idea came from one of my best friends, Laura, who talked to our friend Chloe about it, and they decided they would mention it to me. Despite my shock and grief, I agreed immediately: *Yes, let's do it.*

Before I knew it, my family and friends were all hustling to help get it done. Chumpy's parents had flown over and everyone was there to help. Luckily, because Chumpy's parents were already there and were both on board, we were able to get affidavits done and all the written legal documentation without going through the court.

It was a strange time. Everyone was in complete shock, yet there we all were, signing documents with no idea what was going on. We just knew that if, by some miracle, there was a chance I could have Chumpy's baby, the only time we could do it was now.

In those moments, it felt like Chumpy was pulling strings for us to make it all happen. We got all the documents at the very last minute. We'd found a beautiful doctor from an IVF clinic, and he was literally sitting outside the room waiting to get the documents and the go-ahead. He was the one who went in and retrieved Chumpy's sperm before the time limit was up. Surprisingly, sperm can survive in a deceased person's body for more than seven days after, and luckily my doctor was able to get a healthy sample.

I didn't have time to plan whether I wanted to become a solo mum then and there. I paid to have the sperm put on ice and parked this crazy idea for a while, as I was deep in my grief and couldn't even contemplate the idea of doing it on my own.

I feel so incredibly fortunate that we had the resources and the means to make this happen in such a crucial time. And I know that a lot of widows haven't had this opportunity.

—

After Chumpy's accident, as soon as I discovered I had not naturally fallen pregnant, I knew I was going to try IVF. For the first time, I had a glimmer of hope. I still had to navigate through a lot of grief, but it was the one sure thing I knew – I was going to have this baby. Everyone around me said to wait a little longer, maybe a few years. *What if you meet someone else?* But there was nothing I was more certain of.

When Chloe and I started the *Darling, Shine!* podcast almost a year after Chumpy's passing, things started to move quickly. My online audience grew from people's interest in what had unfolded in my life. It's something that feels quite surreal, knowing that my success and growth began from a devastating loss.

As the podcast continued to grow, I started to feel really empowered. I think it gave me the confidence to feel, like, *You know what? Maybe I could have this baby. Maybe I could really do this on my own.* I have many friends who don't have lots of money. *If they can do it*, I thought, *I know I can do it too.*

I feel very grateful for my financial situation at the time. My dad had given us a sizeable deposit for our house, which meant our mortgage was affordable on a single income. Chumpy and I had worked hard over the years on our savings; I had worked part time and Chumpy was the main breadwinner for our family.

My first round of IVF didn't take, but I was very lucky that the second round worked and brought our daughter, Minnie, into my life. The same doctor saw me through to my pregnancy, and I feel so lucky to have had him. I owe this whole journey to him, my mum and Chloe – but the main person I owe it all to is Chumpy.

To fall pregnant with Chumpy's baby after he'd passed felt bittersweet – to feel excited about the future while still grieving the vision I had for us. At the same time I felt like I was given the greatest gift. It wasn't going to be easy. I was choosing to be mum and dad, but not just any kind of dad: I felt like I needed to become a Chumpy dad, and they felt like huge shoes to fill.

One of the final things I did was change my name to Pullin. While Chumpy and I weren't married, we were tied to each other in every imaginable way. Neither of us cared for marriage or felt it was important, but it was important for me to carry his name and have the same name as our baby.

—

Chumpy and I always had the most incredible and loyal friends. When he passed away, that support only intensified.

Our friends wrapped me in love and care, and I know that if I had been the one who passed, they would have done the same for him.

One of my closest friends, Fish, told my brother shortly after Chumpy's passing, 'I'm going to look after Ellidy. I've got her. We've all got her.' That's exactly how this journey has felt. Fish, Chloe and so many others have been there at every moment, holding me up and supporting Minnie too.

My brother has naturally always had my back. That's just what siblings do – we are each other's rock. He's the best uncle, the fun one Minnie adores. My mum, too, has been incredible, stepping in and helping me navigate life as a solo parent.

One of my closest friends, Tiana, practically became my co-parent, filling a role I never expected her to take on. She's been my rock, my support and my anchor. I honestly don't know where I'd be without her. She's just my person.

I feel so lucky to have this community surrounding me. It's one of the biggest reasons I felt confident enough to take on solo motherhood. Knowing I had so many people in my corner gave me the strength to move forward, even in the darkest moments.

While I have the most incredible community around me, something that surprised me about solo motherhood was the isolating moments during the night. For the first two weeks, my friend stayed with me and really helped me through the night-time feeds and changes, but after those initial nights I was alone. This was when I felt the depths of Chumpy's missing presence the most. While Minnie was up feeding at night, I felt completely alone and it was so incredibly hard and draining. I would wake up so fucking depressed, and exhausted beyond belief.

I think what broke me during those nights was knowing the kind of father Chumpy would have been. We always had an equal relationship where we loved and supported each other, and I just think about how good he would have been as a supportive partner. I know how well he would have looked after me and Minnie, and that he would have been so fucking hands-on and all over that situation like a rash.

Struggling through these early days felt really tough, and I think it's like this for many mums who have been through fertility issues. You are so excited for the baby, and you kind of think that once the baby comes it's going to minimise all the challenges that come with motherhood. And then when that baby comes and you're feeling sleep-deprived, you're like, *Why the fuck am I sad and depressed? I thought this was just going to be the best, all the time.* When I chose to try IVF, I knew that if I got pregnant I would be doing it alone, and I felt like I couldn't complain much – it was a decision that I had chosen to make, and I felt like I had to own that.

There is obviously so much beauty in the whole thing. Minnie looks so much like Chumpy – she has his eyes. I think it's so beautiful. She even has this little chuckle, a really cheeky laugh, that reminds me so much of him. She is also really clean and orderly and likes things a certain way, which is him for sure.

—

I remember once reading an analogy about grief. The size of your grief, its loss and its impact, stays the same. If your grief is, say, the size of a football in your heart, then it will always be the size of a football. But then your life gets bigger and grows around it. You get busy, you start doing things, and your life grows around the grief. So while it looks like the ball gets smaller, it doesn't. It's just that your life gets bigger around it as you grow through it and change and evolve and learn how to manage the grief better.

At the beginning, I used to hate it when I'd hear the phrase, 'Time heals.' I'd think, *Don't you dare fucking tell me time heals. I am climbing Mount Everest to get through this fucking day. Every day sucks.* At first, it feels like time stands still and you can't possibly get through another day. And then, of course, time *does* actually heal. While I would never say that to someone in those early days of grief, I now see that time heals as you literally just have to keep putting one foot in front of the other.

I have learned to manage my grief differently now. When I start to feel it coming on, I make the choice to allow the grief to flow in and out of me in waves, rather than holding it all in and letting it hit me like a fucking tsunami that I'm not expecting. I will go sit on my own and have a big fat cry, or I will talk about it with someone, or plan a therapy session, or book a session with a psychic. I haven't been to a psychic for a while, but it is something that makes me feel connected to Chumpy for a brief moment, and it has helped me so much in the past. It's a release.

I almost welcome the grief now, because I know that by acknowledging it, it helps my healing and I know I will feel better for it later. That's the point where I am at now. I feel stronger.

If there were any words I could offer to a widow who is navigating their grief, I'd say to never stop talking about the person you have lost. Do not shy away from saying their name to your friends and the people around you. Just bring them up.

Don't let them die – let their spirit keep living through you and your stories.

Most importantly, talk to people and get help. Bring people into your world. When you become a widow, you don't know what you're doing. Your friends don't know what they're doing. No one has the tools. Your friends should go easy on you, but you should also go easy on them. Friends might act funny. But the main thing is you don't want to lose them.

At other times, you do have to be alone and crawl into a hole. You have to do it all.

Time does help. Therapy helps – talking, crying, all the feelings and emotions. Let them come up. I promise it helps.

—

For a long time, when I was consumed by my grief, I didn't think it would be possible for me to ever consider finding love again. It's taken years for me to get to a point where I can even see it as a possibility in my future.

I still don't feel ready to have anyone else in my life. I want to be on my own. I want to be with Minnie and focus all of my attention on her. Minnie will always come first, and the rest of the time I want to put my head down and bum up, and I want to grab hold of the opportunities that come my way in any of the spare time I have.

I also know that when the time comes, I can't go looking for what Chumpy and I had. What we had was special. I will make a conscious effort so that the person I choose never feels compared to him.

From the outside, my life now looks full of fun and adventure, but I know all of this has happened because there's a great, enormous loss that I feel in my fucking heart and bones every day. I would give this whole life back in a heartbeat if I knew it could bring Chumpy back to me, but I also accept that I can't do that, so I need to grab everything that comes my way, despite it all. But there's not a moment that goes by that I don't realise Chumpy is missing from my life. I feel the hole in my world every day.

Minnie just loves Chumpy. She calls him 'Chumpy Daddy', and she always picks up photos of him and wants to watch videos of him. She's really drawn to the videos of him jumping into the ocean, swimming and playing guitar. She will squeal, 'Daddy, Daddy!' I will often put on music, and she can identify his songs playing – she's so aware of him now.

I told Minnie that when she goes to sleep, she gets to dream of her dad. Often now, instead of telling me she's tired and wants to go to sleep, she will come to me and say, 'I want to see Daddy now.' In the middle of the night, she often says his name in her sleep, and it's beautiful to think that he is coming to her in a dream.

Minnie has kept his spirit alive for me. Looking at her is a constant reminder that I want to make him proud every day.

MOTHERING ON OUR OWN

JESSICA DOVER
On forgiveness

Journal excerpt, May 2021

It's been three months since my life changed.

Since that day, life has gone fast and slow simultaneously. The past three months have felt long on my own and there have been so many times I've felt sorry for myself, mourning what should have been. It has taken me this long to start feeling somewhat like myself again, and I know I have a long way to go …

Most mothers will separate their lives into two halves: before having their children and after. But for me, the two halves are before I became a single mum and after. It was the moment that everything shattered under me. Life as I imagined it would be altered forever. I always say that becoming a single mum has two parallels: the strength you need to raise your kids on your own, but also the strength they give you to raise them on your own.

I will never forget that day.

I drove home, my mind on autopilot, and pulled into the driveway. My mum was home with my six-month-old son. At the time, Mum was in the early stages of her cancer diagnosis, and I walked in, thinking to myself, *I won't tell her. I don't want her to worry about me. She's got too much to focus her energy on.* But, like any daughter with their mum, as soon as I saw her my eyes welled up and I couldn't hold back my tears. My son was sitting on the playmat, as happy as can be, and I just stood there crying into her arms. I can't imagine what that moment felt like for her. My mum raised my brother and me as a single mum, so she knew this feeling all too well.

That night I drove to my close girlfriend's house. She lived about forty minutes away in a beautiful secluded home in the hills. I just wanted to escape with my son – escape and not process what was really going on. I remember lying in her son's single bed while my son was in and out of the portable cot, breastfeeding all night. That night felt like it lasted for an eternity. Every time I came to, all I could do was picture my son's birth – that moment when we were whole, a family. How did we get here?

I think I cried for two weeks straight. I remember feeding my son in the middle of the night, tears streaming down my face as I held his innocent body against mine. It was my job to protect him and at that moment I didn't know what the future held for us. The stress and emptiness were things I'd never come close to experiencing before. My milk began to dry up and I could barely bring myself to eat – I was nothing like the food lover I usually am. Within fourteen days I was well below my pre-baby weight. I was running on nothing but a fight response mixed in with adrenaline. Complete survival mode.

In those first few weeks, only a few people truly knew the extent of what was going on. As someone who is an overcommunicator with my friends, it shocked me how much I retreated during this time. It felt like communicating with too many people, when I had no answers to give, only magnified the fragile grasp I had on my life as a newly single mum.

Every part of it felt like a mountain. How were my ex-partner and I going to share the time with our son? I was still breastfeeding – I couldn't let him be away from me. Financially it wasn't an option to keep the house, so when would we start discussing how to split it? Where were we going to live now? I knew I was going to have my son full time for the foreseeable future, but how could I manage raising him and financially supporting us?

How, what, when, where repeated in my mind, in every possible scenario.

I wanted answers to everything. I wanted to know what was next and how we were going to do it all. I wanted someone to hand me a road map and say, 'Here, Jess, this is *exactly* how you navigate this.' I would often joke that parenting was like starting a new job you had zero skillsets in. I was still discovering how to be a mum – starting solids, sleep routines – and now I was trying to process the breakdown of a relationship while trying to continue to raise my son to the best of my ability. It felt debilitating, as if I would never be enough.

At the time, my brother was living in Alice Springs, yet as soon as I let him know the news, two days later he flew down to Adelaide to be with me and my son. We didn't do a lot during that week. We went for walks and watched Harry Potter movies, and he helped me with my son as my brain started to catch up on reality.

I remember saying to him that I just wanted to be one year ahead. I wanted to be so far from the reality I was currently facing. Looking back, that makes my heart heavy, as my first year with my son felt stolen from me. You're meant to be soaking up every moment with your new baby at six months, but instead I was barely hanging on. Each day rolled into the other, and I didn't really feel present with anything or anyone. I wished that time away, and it saddens me when I reflect upon it.

Although it all truly feels like a big emotional blur, there were so many significant moments over that time, and conversations that will remain in my brain forever. Like when my girlfriend said to me that nothing needed to be done *today*. 'Things will slowly evolve,' she told me. 'You don't need all the answers right now, as desperately as you may want them. You will grow, your son will grow, and the circumstances will change.'

She was right: things did slowly start working themselves out. It wasn't linear, but what had felt hard one day would feel somewhat easier the next day. I began packing the house up week by week, slowly packing memories and moments away to begin a new life that I hadn't prepared for but knew ultimately was the right decision. The life I had planned in my head as a family was now packed into boxes labelled *Jess's house*. The home I took so much pride in and the nursery I meticulously created for my son just six months earlier, now slowly fading before my eyes. It felt surreal.

My brother offered to move back to Adelaide and live with my son and me. I was grateful for him offering to do this at the time. Now, years on, we're still living together, and words will never articulate what he has done for me – physically, emotionally, mentally and spiritually. I know not everyone will have this option, so I do acknowledge just how fortunate I am that he is a part of my story.

He gifted me space – space in my brain and space in my heart – to begin healing. He will forever be my knight in shining armour, and the most important role model in my life and in my son's. He taught me to forgive, to look at life on a different level, and that the world is bigger than just you or me. The love and respect I have for him is endless and I could never truly repay him for what he's done for us.

We ended up losing our mum two and a half years later from the cancer she was fighting. It was a time I could not have gone through without him by my side.

Things did get easier, yes, but because I chose for them to. It took me about nine months to stop wanting my default emotion to be anger. And, truthfully, I was still angry and upset at the entire situation. But I was exhausted feeling like that. So, I know it sounds simple, but I kept repeating to myself: *I don't want to be angry anymore.*

I was tired of the anger and resentment leaking into other parts of my life. I didn't want to let my past affect my future happiness. That choice was on me – no one else. It did not serve me to hold on to it. I was consciously choosing to be happy again.

Each day I would journal on it, writing down every emotion that surfaced. Some days I felt there were small steps forward and others felt painfully stagnant, but the feeling of anger slowly left my body. Yes, I felt angry and frustrated at times, like every human being, but I chose to look forward. I started dreaming up all the possibilities that life still held for my son and me. And before I knew it, happiness and positivity far outweighed the negatives.

And so began my healing journey, not only for me but for everyone in my life. I learned to be more empathetic, and I began only focusing on what I could control in that moment. I started to have blind faith that things would only get better. I tried to process hard moments or conversations as positively as I could, asking myself: *Could I have approached that situation better? What lesson is this teaching me? Why is this a recurring theme in my life?*

I began detaching from the hardest moments in my past and chose to look forward. I am the happiest I've ever been, my son is happy and I have a good relationship with his dad. I don't regret a moment of it. It changed me for the better. I wouldn't be the person I am today, with the outlook I have, if I didn't go through what I did.

A question someone asked me began a powerful process that has helped me take large steps forward in healing. It was a question about forgiveness. I jumped to my own defence instantly, claiming I wasn't angry and that I was fine. But that question switched on a light bulb in my brain and unlocked pieces I'd never discovered before. So I started to seek out more conversations about forgiveness.

Everyone's traumas and heartbreaks come with pivotal moments that change the path of their stories to come. For me, that act of forgiving – for myself, not for anyone else – instantly lifted a weight off my shoulders.

Acknowledging the pain but forgiving that chapter. Not wishing it away, or wishing that it had never happened. Taking every lesson, big or small, to the next story.

Journal entry, December 2021

What did I learn from this?

- *I learned how all of the strength and resilience I needed was within me all along*

- *How much I don't need anyone else to help me grow*

- *How motivated and driven I am*

- *How excited I am, once the pain stops, to start my next chapter of opportunities*

- *I learned through my own healing process that, rather than seeing forgiveness as a weakness, I can see that there is no greater sign of courage and strength.*

I'm not saying everyone can forgive. I understand the complexities of forgiveness. There are circumstances far different to mine, and actions that some would deem unforgivable. But for me, in my situation, forgiveness was powerful. That's one thing I can pass on to any mothers looking for answers, looking for anything that might make this time pass or feel easier. Look for what you are drawn to, whether that's certain people, a podcast, a yoga class, a book you love or journalling. Try to find what resonates with you, and what you want to explore to help you heal. No one will use the same tools or connect with the same material as you will.

They say things will present themselves to you when you're ready to truly see them. Trust there are certain things standing out to you for a reason. I found this was the case when it came to forgiveness. I was so intrigued that a simple conversation led me down a path of seeking out more conversations around forgiveness in relationships. It meant truly looking at everything from everyone's point of view, and realising that a person's reactions are only a reflection of what they have experienced through their own life or upbringing. This was something I needed to explore. Over time, those little tools and outlooks compounded, and it was incredible to see how powerful they truly were.

Some of my greatest lessons and healings came from conversations with friends, podcasts and journalling. My healing will never stop and I have a long road ahead, but I feel that as long as I am consciously focusing on growing, reflecting and trusting that this is the life I'm meant to be living with my son, everything will work out just as it's meant to.

MOTHERING ON OUR OWN

MARCIA LEONE
On finding the rainbow after the rain

I remember the moment it truly sunk in that I was going to be a solo mum. I was driving to pick up my kids from school and had to pull over. My vision began to blur, and I had pins and needles in my arms. I called my mum through gasping breaths. Isn't it funny how no matter how old we are, we always just want our mum?

I sat on the side of the road, absolute shock and fear flooded my body. Fear for how I would manage the logistics on my own with no family or help nearby; how could I manage two clashing school and sport schedules while running two businesses? Fear of being both the sole provider and the sole nurturer; the pressure of being the only face my children would look for at every sport or school event. But it was the fear of how I would hold my children through their own emotional pain that weighed heaviest on me. Managing their emotions while trying to regulate my own was by far the most challenging part of that season.

Most mums understand the feeling of being nonstop, overwhelmed or touched out, but one of the things that challenged me the most as a solo mum was the fact that you can never tap out. Not even for a minute.

There are so many times when things are flowing and I think, *Wow, I've really got this*. But it can easily be derailed when the curveballs of motherhood hit and you can't share the load.

Especially if you don't have support of family or friends nearby. Simple things I took for granted, like being able to go outside or for a walk around the block on my own when I need a five-minute breather.

I remember being up all night with my daughter when she had a virus. She had been vomiting with a fever, so just had her underwear on. My son had a sport event he couldn't miss, so I carried her to the car wrapped in a blanket for the hour round trip through Sydney traffic. I put her in the car seat asleep with a bucket on her lap. Every five minutes I had to reach back and hold the bucket as she was sick.

On the way home, my car broke down and we had to get out. So there I was, on the side of the road, holding my daughter in her undies, wrapped in a blanket. We eventually got home via a rental car. I had to cancel a job I couldn't deliver that day and lost a lot of income. I remember breaking down in tears thinking, *This is just not sustainable for one person*.

But somehow, we wipe our tears and keep going, right?

I always try to focus on the good things that come with the honour of raising these beautiful children, but some days we just have to throw our hands in the air and surrender to what is a really shitty day, week, month …

I can keep talking about the struggles and challenges over the past four years. I can speak to the times I cried to the child support officer over the broken system, the guilt I felt when my kids came home from their first day at new schools and both hated it. The financial pressures of having to slow down my business because my kids needed me at home. The exhaustion of trying to overcompensate so my children didn't feel like they were missing anything. And the many times I locked myself in the bathroom and cried, 'I just can't do this.' But in every challenge, I found strength; in every heartbreak, a glimmer of hope. Even in the toughest seasons, I found so much joy and gratitude for my little family of three – and for me, the woman inside the mother. Honouring her, nourishing her and prioritising her so I can show up for my kids has been my silver lining.

Today, four years on, I sit in my new home, with a beautiful partner and our kids playing outside. But it's no 'knight in shining armour' or 'happy ending' story. There are challenges in this season, too – merging families has its own joys, and its own set of things that we need to navigate, and that is part of this messy, beautiful life.

But I'm proud of every season we get through as mothers. I'm proud that I trusted my inner knowing, that I was brave enough to make hard choices to take us to this moment. And I wouldn't change any of the journey to get to where we are today.

For the mums at the beginning of their single-mum journey, I would say this: trust that everything is happening for your highest good. The universe will send you signs and push you in situations – often what you're looking for is on the other side of fear.

Even through (especially through!) the toughest times and the most mundane days, look for the glimmers – those everyday snippets that send a sense of gratitude through your body.

Fill your own cup. Take time to do things you love. Enjoy your freedom. Nourish your friendships. One of the silver linings of becoming a single mum was connecting with others who are going through the same situation. That sense of sisterhood – someone who understands what you are going through – is so important. If I hadn't experienced the loneliness of being a single mum, I wouldn't have launched my retreats for mothers. Sharing parts of my experiences has not only resonated with other women, but for some been their survival guide.

Date yourself first. I didn't even think of dating anyone for almost two years. My focus was on healing and my children. Become the best version of yourself. Have fun. Be a fun mum for your kids.

Remember, it's the most challenging moments that bring the most growth. As the saying goes, 'You can't have the rainbow without a little rain.'

Your children are lucky to have you, and you them.

Enjoy the journey and trust that the best is yet to come. Because it is. Xx

MOTHERING ON OUR OWN

NATASHA ROFE
On embracing life after loss

I always knew I wanted to be a mum. It was the one thing I desired more than anything else in the world. The thought of nurturing a little life, guiding them through their ups and downs, and showering them with unconditional love was a dream I clung to dearly.

After struggling to conceive naturally, my husband and I turned to IVF. When we discovered that our first round was successful, 'ecstatic' was an understatement. I was overjoyed to finally see my dream of becoming a mum come true. From the outside, my life appeared perfect – a loving husband, a beautiful home, a successful career and now a baby on the way. But behind closed doors, the reality was far from the picture-perfect life I projected.

My marriage felt toxic, and I was deeply depressed. I held on to the hope that this beautiful blessing of a child would be the answer to my sadness, the light that would dispel the darkness surrounding me.

The day Sonny was born was the greatest day of my life.

I remember feeling as if I was the only woman in the world who had ever given birth, and I was filled with immense pride in what my body had created. But that euphoria was short-lived.

It wasn't long before the crushing weight of depression and the suffocating environment of my marriage pulled me back under. The 'baby bubble' that so many women talk about – this magical time of sunshine and rainbows – never came for me. Instead, I felt disconnected and trapped, unable to experience the joy I had anticipated.

As the years went by, the depression deepened, and I knew that if I wanted any semblance of a life, I had to leave my marriage. Leaving was one of the hardest things I've ever done. I walked away with no sense of self, no confidence – those had been stripped from me long ago.

I was terrified.

How was I going to survive on my own? I felt like the most inadequate mother. How could I possibly raise my child and give him the love he deserved when I felt so empty?

I vividly remember the night I left. I was so scared but numb at the same time. I knew my life was about to change in unimaginable ways, but I had no idea just how difficult the road ahead would be.

If you've been in a toxic relationship, you'll understand the ramifications. I felt constantly undermined, controlled and was told I wasn't a good mother. Unfortunately, I believed every one of those lies.

After a year of therapy and working through my self-doubt, I slowly began to undo the years of lies that had been fed to me. I started to believe that I was a good mum and that I could provide my child with everything he needed. But I also realised that I needed to rewrite the dreams I had for my life.

As I began to navigate what this new life looked like, the weight of my responsibilities lingered. Here I am, a single mum, feeling lonely and isolated, financially struggling and completely overwhelmed. I often look at Sonny with a deep sense of guilt. I can't give him everything I want to – holidays, toys, trips to the movies. There are days when he spends hours watching TV or playing with his toy soldiers alone while I work from home. Our weekly dinner dates consist of him ordering chicken nuggets and chips, while I order nothing – not because I'm not hungry, but because I can't afford it.

The anxiety and worry are constant companions. Am I present enough for him? Does he know I'd rather be spending time with him than working? Will he grow up with issues because he didn't get enough attention from me?

But I have no choice. I need to work to keep us afloat.

—

One day, I got a phone call no one should ever receive. My brother was dead. My beautiful twenty-seven-year-old brother – the father of my little nephew, Archie, and engaged to Emma, his partner – had become a victim of his own depression and ended his life.

I thought I had experienced heartbreak before, but I was wrong. The pain of losing my brother was unlike anything I had ever felt. This life-changing event not only shattered my world but also deeply affected my entire family.

The story of losing my brother could fill another chapter, but I want to keep this brief. His passing changed me in profound ways. The things I once cared about – growing my business, earning more money, chasing status – suddenly seemed trivial. I realised that life is to be lived right now – even in its imperfect, tough, exhausting, lonely and overwhelming moments.

Life doesn't stop.

Being a single mum doesn't stop.

The hardships will always be there, and I can't change that. But what I can change is the negative-thinking loop in my brain. Life isn't perfect, but it is beautiful.

After my brother's passing, I decided that I didn't want to live another day wishing away my current situation. Yes, I am tired, but I also have air in my lungs. Yes, I doubt myself, but I also have the sweetest, most kind-hearted child. Yes, money is tight, but I truly have everything I need.

This mental shift felt almost seamless. I had wasted so many years holding my breath, waiting for life to 'improve' before enjoying the moment, before being thankful, before allowing myself to be happy. But I've come to realise that time may never come. Learning to be still and present in what today brings has brought true contentment and peace into my life. And although I would do anything to see my brother again, I have him to thank for this lesson.

Regardless of how dark times can be, there is beauty in every moment. We are never truly alone. These feelings of overwhelm and anxiety plague us all at one point or another, and that's okay. But if, for just a moment, we can stop, take a breath and look around at the life we are living right now, we might find that it's more beautiful than we ever realised.

And so I choose to embrace the chaos, the exhaustion, the uncertainty. I choose to see the beauty in the struggle, to cherish the moments of joy, no matter how small they may seem. It's not about chasing an ideal life, but about finding contentment in our reality.

MONTANA LOWER
On finding a village

I never planned to be a single mum. Like many, I had dreamed of starting a family since I was a little girl. A family where things would be different. A family that would last a lifetime. Like many, I thought love was all you needed to make things work. And yet, like many, I came to the humble realisation that love comes in many forms, and sometimes loving looks like letting go in order to create a more peaceful environment for a child to grow up in.

I became a single mother amid the long and complicated miscarriage of my second child. After two months of bleeding and trying to allow my body to release the pregnancy naturally, I finally opted for surgical support to complete the process. By this time, I was so frail in both body and spirit that I could barely walk or work. I knew I had a long road of recovery ahead of me and it was more important than ever to be in an environment that supported that.

Choosing to leave in a time when I *so desperately* needed support was no easy choice.

Ending a relationship rarely is, especially when there are children involved. Yet it was when I met the edges of myself that I really asked myself the hard questions: *Am I really getting what I need out of this relationship to be the mother and woman I want to be in this world? Is this the environment I want to raise my child in? Should I leave while we only have one child? Is this just a phase? Should I just stick it out until my child is older?*

Martyrdom runs rife in the world of motherhood. It latches its claws on to you and says, 'How dare you consider your own needs above your child's?' To which I say: happy and healthy parents in two separate homes is better than two miserable parents in one.

I didn't really know what I was signing myself up for with single parenting. It felt like a matter of just putting one foot in front of the other. It was in this time that the women in my life really stepped up to take care of me. I have found myself living with women for most of my time as a single parent. This has been the silver lining among it all. Living with women has enclosed me in a blanket of sweetness and nurturing that my little girl and I needed to establish ourselves in the world again.

With women, there is an ease and understanding of what is required to take care of someone at a foundational level. When little voices are heard crying through the night, there is a hot drink waiting on the kitchen bench in the morning. There is always someone ready to build a puzzle or make potions with my daughter while I get dressed. There is always dinner on the stove – sometimes multiple dinners to choose from (which is great for a fussy four-year-old). There is a softness and inherent taking care of each other that hums through the home and recalibrates healing hearts with the deep understanding that it is our birthright to have our needs met, and how easeful it can be to meet them for each other.

It sounds beautiful, doesn't it? Idyllic, even. And this part of my single parenting is. Thank god, because in the wake of rebuilding myself after what I have known to be my biggest heartbreak yet, it has felt like most of the time I've just been trying to hold it together. In these times I have been so grateful for my healing practices (breathwork, therapy and kinesiology), my friends and family for every kind of support, my business and my team for keeping me afloat, and my ever-growing heart for paving the way forward and guiding me as life unfolds in beautiful ways I never could have imagined.

As I write this, I feel grief – not only for the family I once hoped for, but the wishes I had for our co-parenting. But I trust that we are still at the start of a very long road. It is my belief that co-parenting can be done peacefully when parents are able to prioritise the children's needs above their pain, and when they can show up with consistency, clear communication, aligned values and respect. There is no reason why a child shouldn't be able to thrive in these circumstances. I maintain the vision that we can make this possible for our daughter.

RENEE STASKA
On mothering through adversity

After my first child was born, the cracks in my relationship started to form. I was a stay-at-home mum, and my partner started to work very late and on weekends. Six months after our son was born, my partner came home and told me he had been struggling to get through the work day. He explained that the pressure of providing for our little family was too much.

He was having issues that I had not been privy to, so when he came to me, it was a big shock. It felt like the beginning of the end, but soon afterwards I fell pregnant with my daughter. I thought, *Well, okay, now we really need to make this work.*

Things in our relationship got worse throughout my pregnancy and eventually I packed up my things and I went to my mum's house. We had lots of conversations and I was given professional advice that made it clear that I had to leave. While I knew it was the safest thing for my children, at the same time I was desperate for us to remain a family.

I moved into a place of my own after our second child was born. I wish I could say that I never went back to my partner, but I didn't feel strong enough to completely cut him off. So I let him enter our lives once again, and I held on to the hope that things would get better.

We went back and forth in this horrible cycle, until two years later I unexpectedly fell pregnant with our third child. This became the deciding point for me: I wasn't going to stay in this any longer. I wasn't going to allow another baby to go through this.

A simple growth scan twenty-eight weeks into my pregnancy would flip my entire world on its head.

My other children had both been small, so this was an extra scan to check my son was growing okay. After the scan, I was pulled into a side room and asked to wait for a doctor. Naively, I assumed this baby was just following suit, and that I'd be told he was small and needed more monitoring.

Instead, I was informed by the doctor that my little darling had a condition called ascites. Basically, he had fluid inside his abdomen that shouldn't have been there. I was told, 'Your baby is not compatible with life.'

I drove back to my mum's house with my mind in a blur. He had been fine at twenty weeks, and had passed that screening without so much as a blip.

The hospital staff told me to head into the Women's and Children's Hospital the next day for more extensive scanning. I hoped that we'd arrive and find there had been a mistake but unfortunately the next scan was the same. He had the fluid build-up, and they weren't sure why. I was told that, at twenty-eight weeks pregnant, medical abortions were not available and the best they could offer was some testing to prepare me for the future. They were honest with me: if I made it to full term, my baby was likely to be stillborn.

My mum drove me to the hospital for the next ten uncertain weeks. Slowly, the ascites started to go down, but his little liver, spleen and heart were working overtime to try to get rid of the fluid. I was offered an amniocentesis – a test that could potentially give a genetic answer to why this was happening. It wouldn't change anything but with no straws to grab, I went ahead.

The amniocentesis didn't find anything. So, at thirty-eight weeks, I was induced and he arrived safely, looking just like his big brother, with blond fuzz and almost exactly the same size. He did have a larger tummy but otherwise he was divine.

Quickly, he was whisked away to the special care unit. My mum went with him as my birth had been a whirlwind and I had lost a lot of blood. When I got to see him next, his little body was covered in wires – oxygen, heart monitors – and little bandaids. He had some blood taken so they could run more tests. After a few days in the special care unit, he was able to be in my room. It felt so surreal having my tiny treasure in my arms after what had felt like an eternity wondering what would happen to him.

He had an enlarged tummy, but the only other remarkable find was that he had high liver enzymes. The care team thought this was because his liver had been working overtime to clear the fluid out of his abdomen. We were placed under the care of the gastroenterology team and sent on our way.

Bringing him home was so exciting. He was instantly adored by his doting big brother and sister. He felt like a miracle after so much stress. He was a calm and happy baby, with eyes that looked straight into mine as if he knew me so well.

Days at home with my darling. Enjoying the snuggles and the never-ending feeds. Watching how his eyes fixated on mine and his little hand reached out to me, just to check I was there. What a blessing it is to be a little person's safe home.

Within six months, our perfect little world began to crack.

I was called into the doctor's office and told that the gene panel test had come back. My little man had Niemann-Pick disease type C1. It was fatal and had no cure. The doctor urged me not to google it, as I would only read horrible things. He told me to take him home and love him as he would be lucky to see his fifth birthday.

When I got back to my mum's house, I repeated what I was told and crumbled into pieces. My baby boy. How could this be his fate? What had I done wrong by him? I can't quite put into words how surreal that felt.

A few short months later, I met with a new team of doctors called the metabolic team. They were able to tell me more about his condition. After finding out that this was a genetic condition passed on through me and the children's dad, I opted to get my two older children blood-tested to rule out the possibility of them having it too.

When both my older children's tests came back positive, I felt my heart physically break. I cried and cried and held on to my baby, wishing the ground would swallow me up. I was introduced to palliative care. There was nothing more they could do for us. My baby, who wasn't quite one, my two-year-old and my four-year-old had all been declared terminally ill.

I felt like my world ended on that very day. It seemed impossible to take another breath without my chest caving in. I truly couldn't understand how the world was still spinning when my reality had been shattered into millions of pieces.

Of course, at this point I reached back out to the children's father. I told him about the diagnoses and how I felt lost, not knowing what to do. I told him that I desperately needed him to sort his shit out because I really needed him to come back. How on earth could I do this all on my own?

Unfortunately, he couldn't pull himself together to do this.

As a solo mum of three, I had no option but to get up and keep going. My babies were so young and so reliant on me, and I couldn't let them down. I crawled out of that dark space and faced this new reality head-on. Life had to move forward. I couldn't break down. I couldn't just sit on the couch and cry because I had to get up for my children. I guess that's just what mums do: they keep on keeping on, even when they don't want to. By no means was it easy – I still have days that feel so soul-crushingly hard – but as much as everything had changed, at the same time nothing had changed at all.

I decided to make a promise to myself: that my babies would know no different. All I had ever wanted was to be a mum. And although my heart was broken, it was still so full of love. My kids deserved a happy mum who helped them make the most of every day.

Tomorrow is never promised, so now we live for today. We love hard and splash about in life and face everything together. Us against all odds.

ABBY GILMORE
On a new family bond

I became a mother at twenty-one. I was a young woman filled with dreams of creating the perfect family I had always yearned for. I wanted so deeply to be needed, to love something unconditionally. Looking back, I realise that my desire to have children so early stemmed from my own fear of abandonment, a need to fill the void with something that was mine. But motherhood, like life, does not follow a script. My journey brought with it the rawness of pain, the sharp sting of judgement from others, and the challenge of co-parenting while maintaining my children's sense of love and security.

I had my second daughter, Arlo, just twenty-one months after my first daughter, Milla, but when she was just six weeks old, my world came crashing down around me. I was confronted by infidelity – a revelation that shattered my dreams and left me grasping for a sense of normalcy. The pain robbed me of so many precious memories, especially during

Arlo's first year. I find myself needing to be gentle with myself about this, recognising how intense pain and the pressure of an unravelling relationship made it hard to hold on to the beautiful moments amid the chaos.

My ex-partner is a high-profile AFL (Australian rules football) player, and our private pain quickly became public. The news broke everywhere – on TV, in the newspapers and across the internet. Headlines were written to cause damage. I wish I could go back and support myself through that time better; people I trusted certainly took advantage of me. I did the best I could in those times, considering the circumstances, but I was quite literally going through my sadness with what felt like the whole world watching. Weirdly, that's also where I found some comfort – by connecting with other women who had walked this path before me.

Thrown into the deep end, I faced the scrutiny of the media, who turned my personal struggles into a public spectacle. I was a young woman trying to navigate a life that was suddenly under a magnifying glass. But even then, I reminded myself that my superpower was to share my message, not my mess, while all eyes were on me. It was a lesson in resilience – learning to focus on what truly mattered, even when it felt like all eyes were on my relationship breakdown and people were just waiting for me to fail.

I can still recall the smiles I forced for the camera, the cheerful words I spoke in interviews, all while hiding the darkest secret of my life: that inside I was dying, knowing that everything was on the brink of collapse. That secret, that internal battle, left me feeling like I was losing myself. But motherhood taught me that my worth wasn't tied to a man or anyone else. It was inside me all along. My children have been my mirrors, reflecting to me the parts of myself I had forgotten – the parts I learned to protect so fiercely as a young girl. They helped me reconnect with who I was before the world tried to mould me into something different.

Re-partnering has brought a new layer of complexity to my journey as a mother. With two daughters from my previous relationship and a son with my current partner, I often find myself navigating the delicate balance of ensuring that every child feels equally valued and loved. There's a constant awareness within me, a hyperfocus on making sure our language and love are always inclusive, never dividing. I'm mindful that my daughters might feel different because their father isn't here, while my son sees his dad every day. I strive to create an environment where none of them feels like an outsider, where the love we share feels like a bond that connects us all, regardless of how our family came together.

My partner has been a constant source of support, offering patience and understanding as we navigate these dynamics together. He brings a calm presence and a steady love that has helped me feel secure in our journey. He understands the complexities and never shies away from the challenges, always striving to build a home where all our children feel like equal parts of our family.

It's not easy. I'm constantly checking myself, making sure my actions and words make each child feel seen and secure. I've become sensitive to the smallest cues, aware of how easily they could feel left out or different. Blending our family has taught me that being a mother in this context means redefining what it means to be whole. It's about creating a home where love is the language that binds us, always making room for everyone.

Motherhood was not just about nurturing my children but relearning the values that were buried deep within me: discipline, hard work, and resilience. Every day, I face my fears, no longer living in the shadow of failure. I ask my kids, 'How many mistakes did you make today?' and we talk openly about feelings and emotions. I am not afraid of their big feelings because I've learned to be at peace with my own. I try to look at them with empathy and curiosity, guiding them back to safety instead of judgement. I know they are having their own experiences, separate from mine, and that's okay.

Reflecting on those early days, I remember the power struggles I felt as a new mother – the weight of past generations of mothers who unknowingly passed on their experiences and expectations. I felt the pressure to conform to traditions, to follow advice that often conflicted with my instincts. I remember the constant barrage of voices telling me what to do, what to give up, and how to be a mother. But deep down, all I wanted was to keep my babies close, to protect them, to hold on to that gut instinct that so many others tried to sway. I wish I had known then what I know now – that it's okay to trust myself, to listen to my instincts, and to ask for love and support, not just for my babies' needs but for my own as well.

Through all of this, I've learned that life's pain and suffering lead to growth and understanding. Nothing happens by accident. I want other mothers to see their strength and capability through my story. To know that, despite the struggles, we are always growing, always finding new ways to heal, and always learning to trust ourselves. Every experience is an opportunity to reconnect with the strength that lies within us.

MOTHERING ON OUR OWN

JACINTHA FIELD
On becoming your own hero

Wearing the label *single mother* wasn't part of the plan. But life pushes us in unexpected directions, testing our resilience in ways we never thought possible.

In 2019, I separated from the father of my child. I'd love to say it was a conscious separation, one of those beautiful love stories that ended with blissful love, like Gwyneth Paltrow and Chris Martin's 'conscious uncoupling'. But that wasn't my reality. In the blink of an eye, my world shattered. It felt like I had been hit by a semitrailer, shattering into a million pieces. I wasn't just separating from a partner; I was walking away from a life I had always known. It was brutal. Everything happened so quickly that I barely had time to catch my breath.

Within weeks of the separation, I received legal letters from some of the most expensive lawyers in Melbourne. So there I was, a single mother, broke, a full-time carer for my son with no job and no money, and living in what felt like

Timbuktu, far away from friends. My phone was cut off, and my child was a mess.

And just when you think it couldn't get any worse, it did, like a tornado of pain ripping through the sky. Not only did the stress cause me to lose all my hair – something that had been such a massive part of my identity – but it felt like my very essence was being torn apart. And yet the pain didn't end there. In 2020, my son, Axel, started school, Covid hit, and the separation process was in full swing. My son was not okay. He was jumping out of the car, throwing bins around the house, and running up the street because he was trying to escape his feelings. And I could hardly blame him because I felt like I wanted to do the same.

I wanted to curl into a ball and not have to wake up again. I was angry. Why was this happening to me? I had been on a spiritual journey for the past five years; I'd thought I was doing all the right things, and I couldn't understand the brutality of this situation.

My way of coping with pain is, first, to talk it out with whatever ear will listen, and then, when the shame of oversharing sets in, to isolate myself. Though I may appear to be an extrovert, deep down I'm an introvert who needs to piece together the puzzle of my emotions. I need time. And I need space. I have learned to sit in my shit. But I quickly realised that pulling away from others was triggering for those around me. They needed answers, and I didn't have them. Break-ups take two to tango; it's never just one person's fault.

Over the summer, I taught my son how to ride a bike. Watching him gain confidence and joy on two wheels was a triumph for me as a mother. We had plenty of 'yippee' moments and fist pumps. But those moments were quickly ripped in two. When I became a mother, I had envisioned countless joyful moments, like riding bikes together as a family. But that dream was cut short before it even had a chance to begin.

The moment your child meets their potential stepmum is devastatingly difficult. We were still grieving; I wasn't ready for this. It all happened too quickly. Despite all my efforts getting my son bike-ready, his first family bike ride was with my ex-partner and his new girlfriend on their first meeting. That moment brought me to my knees. It was one of the most challenging days of the separation. I reached out to two of my closest girlfriends for comfort, but neither responded. I sat at home alone, consumed by agonising despair, wondering how my life had come to this. I felt so worthless.

After listening to therapist Marisa Peer, I found a ring engraved with *I AM ENOUGH*. It reminded me daily that I had everything I needed within me. After years of placing my self-worth in the hands of others, I finally understood that true love starts with your relationship with yourself. The ring became my anchor, and I repeated its message whenever I doubted my worth. It cemented my commitment to rediscovering who I was and embracing every part of my journey.

—

Amid my pain, I did what I did best – I searched for solutions. I read every book I could, listened to as many podcasts as possible, and chewed the ear off anyone who would listen. But after six months of grieving, people began to stop listening. I was too much; it was too much. I couldn't breathe. All I wanted was someone to bring me ice cream, hold me and let the tears flow. No matter how much I tried to rely on others to help me process my grief, I came to realise that not everyone could hold space for my big emotions.

You can't expect someone who hasn't been through their own storm to walk with you through yours. And even if they have, every situation is different. Mine had as many layers as an onion.

By the six-month mark, it hadn't even touched the sides of what was to come.

I had to be the one to pick up the pieces, for myself and for my son. At almost forty, I knew that this was my responsibility. I didn't want anyone else carrying my burden. It was up to me to protect myself and to heal. My ex-partner and I didn't belong together; I knew that to my core. We saw life differently, but that didn't mean it wouldn't still hurt.

I had spent years teaching others how to build resilience through adversity and pain, and now I was being tested in the most profound way. Years of childhood trauma, break-ups, domestic violence from a past relationship, and generational pain were surfacing all at once. It was time to face them.

I knew that I had to heal fully before moving forward to break the patterns from my past relationships. That meant spending a lot of time on my own. But to be honest, I was scared. The world became scary to me. There were many times I wanted to give up. There was so much betrayal. For years, I hid away.

Before the separation, I had quit drinking because it didn't align with my soul. If there was ever a time to start drinking again, it was now. But I held on to my truth. I was also very cautious not to jump straight into another relationship. I needed to discover the part I had played in this mess. I have a pattern of co-dependency in relationships – a trait I wanted to smash to pieces. So I needed to discover its root cause.

During my healing journey, I immersed myself in breathwork, pranayama and tantra, joining a year-long mentorship program to deepen my understanding of these practices. I became a meditation teacher to learn the art of forgiveness – but facing that while still holding on to so much anger was incredibly difficult. The first step in forgiveness is feeling the anger and letting it go, but that was easier said than done. My mantra was 'trust the process'.

Forgiveness sets you free; it doesn't excuse the other person's behaviour. I wasn't ready to teach – I became a meditation teacher for survival. I also studied reiki, not just to calm my nervous system but Axel's as well. He was also feeling the effects of the separation, and it was my role to guide him through it. I consulted with a number of psychologists, psychotherapists, psychics and healers – I trusted that I was guided to where I needed to heal. On days when it all became too much, my dear psychics gave me hope and a spring in my step. They got me through the day. I took everything with a grain of salt, but it's incredible how spot-on they were. Many 'no frickin' way!' moments came true.

One of the hardest things to process was the number of people who didn't show up for me. As a single mother struggling through some of the darkest days, I was shocked by how few people checked in. Even my family wasn't there for me as I had hoped. But, as life often does, this taught me one of my greatest lessons: *No one is showing up to save you.*

You go from feeling utterly broken to becoming your own Wonder Woman, learning to stand alone, finding strength and solace in yourself, and continuing despite it all. And that has been the greatest gift.

They say divorce and moving house are two of life's greatest stresses. I did both in the same year. I moved to the coast, not knowing anyone, to be near Mother Earth and to heal my soul. The coast was our healing centre – all while homeschooling Axel during a global pandemic. There wouldn't be any day-to-day support for another four years. It allowed me to reinvent myself, but it was the hardest thing I've ever had to do.

—

I call separation 'the mud'; you must go through it to come out the other side. In the mud of separation, when everything felt stuck, I learned to stop fearing the judgement of others and to show up authentically. I cried for more than a year, releasing years of pent-up pain with each tear. I made mistakes and said silly things, but I forgave myself. I was hurting.

Then, one day, the puzzle pieces slowly came back together, but they aligned in a new way. I emerged as a stronger version of myself, with newfound self-belief. New friends entered my life, and my smile grew brighter. I began living in a way that was more aligned to my values than ever before. I discovered the importance of boundaries, learned to speak up and started trusting my intuition. I stopped accepting breadcrumbs and, as a reformed people-pleaser, I found my true worth. I created a life surrounded by nature and filled with joy, and found freedom in simple pleasures.

As a human, I need connection, growth and belonging. I need to be seen, heard and valued to feel safe. Something that has helped me immensely is what my psychologist once said to me: 'Other people's opinions of you are just that – their opinions. It doesn't mean that it's true.'

So I learned to let people talk, knowing that I knew the truth. I didn't feel the need to share my side of the story. If something felt off, I distanced myself from that person. My intuition became my guiding light.

What I found worked well with Axel was the expression of colour and art. He was too little to express his feelings, so we used art. When he had difficulty registering emotions, we would get a piece of paper and draw circles. I would then ask him to put faces in these circles about his feelings. He would draw sad, disappointed and angry faces. Then we attached a colour to these emotions. For example, blue was often sad, red was angry and green was disappointed. Next, I would ask him to feel each feeling and explain why he felt this way. This process gave him space and time to feel what he was feeling and the strength to express it with love and support.

The person I am most grateful to is Axel. He has taught me unconditional love, and I've shown him strength. Together, we are a team. I am his warrior, always there to protect and guide him. Through our bond, he has learned that feeling big emotions is okay, and that I'll be there for him no matter what. I encourage him to be his true, authentic self around me.

As a family and child counsellor, I now guide children and parents in managing big emotions, fostering self-regulation and cultivating self-love. Art and play therapy are central to my approach, helping children express themselves and build confidence by embracing their true selves. I focus on understanding and processing emotions, highlighting what needs to be released from the body.

By normalising feelings and viewing tantrums as signs of dysregulation, we turn these moments into opportunities for learning self-regulation. Guiding parents to develop self-love and self-compassion nurtures a supportive home environment. I also encourage parents to help their children build emotional 'forcefields' to shield against unwanted words and reflect on how others' feelings impact them, fostering emotional intelligence and resilience.

—

Separations are awful. I won't pretend otherwise. But I've learned that the universe doesn't give you anything you can't handle. If you're not right with someone, it's time to let them go. When one door closes, another opens, as long as you've learned the lessons. Something better is always waiting on the other side – and often, that's the strongest, most powerful version of you.

In the end, my journey wasn't about finding someone else. It was about finding myself. Becoming your own hero means embracing every challenge, every heartbreak and every moment of joy. I had to learn to love myself, flaws and all, knowing that I was enough and that you're never too much for the right people. I invite you to step into your inner Wonder Woman too.

MOTHERING ON OUR OWN

ELIZABETH ANILE
On making lemonade

My intuition had known for some time that something wasn't quite right. Despite his repeated denials, and his insistence that everything was in my head, I knew it wasn't. But I wanted to believe him. Because I thought my baby boy needed his dad around. Because I was twenty-six and doing this alone was simply not an option. So I grabbed a shovel and buried my gut instinct with a dense layer of fresh soil as I convinced myself he was right. I was oversensitive. I was exhausted. I was delusional.

'This is all in your head,' he'd reassure me, soothing my insecurities and stroking my face. Those were the good days, when burying myself was easy. It was much harder when that very hand stiffened into a sharply pointed finger, threatening the same face he'd just cradled. He told me he loved me. What more did I need? So I'd tell him to grab a shovel and smooth another scoop of dirt, until eventually the confident, vivacious, headstrong woman I had once been slowly suffocated and disappeared. Little did I know that just after the clock struck midnight on one fateful April night, I'd have my chance to dig my way out.

My eight-month-old son, Ollie, stirred earlier than usual – a sign, in hindsight, that this night wouldn't follow the familiar rhythm of every other one before it. Once I'd rocked Ollie back to sleep, I returned to our room and was tucking myself in when I saw it. His phone, unlocked, wide awake beside his sleeping body. He'd fallen asleep to a podcast but somehow, for a reason I'll never understand, his phone hadn't auto-locked as it usually would. We'd entered a twilight zone where right was left and up was now down.

One message was enough to tear the book of my life in two, never to be glued back together again, signifying to the reader we'd crossed over from Before Affair to After Affair.

All these years later, when I close my eyes I can still see myself writhing on the bedroom floor. Clutching my belly. Gasping for air, yet somehow moaning, bleating in a foreign, animalistic wail, thinking, *Is this what it feels like to die?* If it was, I desperately begged for it to end soon, my body contorting as I beckoned the white light to descend and lure me in with the promise of a blissful release from this trench of eternal hell. It may sound awfully melodramatic, but many people who have been blindsided by infidelity shares a similar tale.

While my memory now is blurry, I recall feeling grateful that Ollie was asleep, his bedroom door like an airbag shielding him from the fallout. My heart wasn't just breaking for me, it was breaking for my baby too. He had no idea that the course of his life had just changed forever. When I saw that text, I knew it was over. In a matter of moments, I realised I didn't know this man at all.

As autumn rain battered the bedroom window, he packed a bag and left. A voice from somewhere told me to pick myself up off the floor. So I did. It told me to get back into bed. So I did. It told me to keep staring at the little green light in the bathroom to distract me from the torturous loop of images of them together. So I did. It told me I wanted to write about being a young mum. So here is my story.

As dawn broke, Ollie woke – much earlier than usual – to this new, alternate reality. *It's only me here.* The weight of our home's emptiness was crushing. I had to get up. There was quite literally no other choice.

My feet touched the floor, but my legs could barely walk. Weak, shaking, like Bambi taking his first steps, I glimpsed my face in the hallway mirror – pale, pained and utterly unrecognisable. I opened Ollie's bedroom door. There he was: my future, my reason, my hope, beaming the most beautiful smile I'd ever seen as he caught my eye. I scooped him into my arms, and with the first words I'd uttered in hours, I apologised from the depths of my soul. I explained that his whole world had just changed. But it was okay, I told him, because Mummy was here. And she loved him. And I would forevermore.

With that, the two of us emerged from his bedroom and quite literally stepped into our new reality, where it was just the two of us. That morning, Ollie's pure, unconditional love saved me. It empowered me with the strength to haul myself out of the shallow grave I was disappearing within. From that moment, I had to find a way to keep going. I had to show, through my actions, that I was paving a new path and breaking the well-worn family patterns once and for all. This cycle was ending now. Ollie was going to be a man one day. What kind of man did I hope he would be?

With every step forward and giant leap back, I tenaciously set about creating the life I always imagined we'd have. The following few years were undoubtedly the most challenging of my life. In parallel with my little family crumbling, a greater, deeper, darker force also tore apart my family of origin. My stomach still drops as I reflect on the great amount of pain, grief and fear that enveloped my world for what felt like an endless amount of time. There were moments when I didn't know if I could keep going.

But among the chaos, those years were equally electrifying, revolutionary, life-changing. I watched my son grow from a small, smushed, premature baby who was taken off me moments after he was born, into a beautiful, strong-willed, sensitive soul who cracks me up daily, inspires me with his courage, and leaves me in awe of his empathy. He looks at me like I'm magic, loves me unconditionally, and encourages me to look up and see the rainbow on a rainy day.

He taught me how to put one foot in front of the other before he could even walk himself. He showed me how important it was to use my voice before he knew how to talk. He is my world. He is the love of my life. Everything that happened that fateful night happened exactly as it was supposed to. My 'fairytale life' needed to be brutally dismantled so I could rebuild every building block of my life.

And as my son grew, so did I. With extensive therapy, I evolved. This metamorphosis forced me to re-evaluate what I was willing to put up with. Suddenly the qualities I had once accepted were now intolerable. The treatment I used to turn a blind eye to was now inexcusable. I wouldn't be half the woman I am today without this experience. Being a single mum has taught me I am strong, resourceful, capable, resilient and courageous. There is no one to rely on during the overnight fevers or to fall back on if work runs late and I miss pick-up, or to help prepare dinner while I tend to a million other things. I bear the brunt of all the responsibility, all the time. And sure, that can be challenging, but it's also among the things I admire most within myself.

I never, ever thought I'd be able to do the things I do all by myself and live the life I live. But I can. And I do. And I thrive. And, most importantly, my son is thriving too.

In those early days, I launched a blog about my experiences, then a podcast called *Lemonade*. The lemon became my motif. I had one tattooed on my wrist to remind me to keep turning these lemons into sweet lemonade. Single mothers would reach out to me daily, and through this I realised how fulfilling it was helping other women.

I quit my career in journalism and went back to university to study a Master of Counselling while juggling two jobs, a pandemic and raising my son. Now, I run my own psychotherapy practice, where I sit with people experiencing myriad challenges. However, there's no feeling like the one I have when a newly single mum books in and collapses on my couch. She looks up at me, sometimes crying, often pleading for some kind of solution to take this pain away. Chills ripple through my body as I look back at her and see myself. I get it. I know her. I am her, just several years down the track. And I wouldn't be opposite her if I hadn't dug myself out of that pit that morning and decided I wanted something different for my life.

This is my lemonade. Because if I've been through all of that, I may as well make it fricking worth it.

AMIE ROHAN
On holding on to hope

My name is Amie Rohan.

I'm a mum of three girls, two here earthside and one angel baby watching over us from above.

I live on the south coast of Victoria. I'm a big lover of the ocean, and living by the coast for me is a must.

I grew up in south-west Victoria, on a farm, with my three siblings. I loved dancing and playing netball, and it was at the local netball club that I met the guy who would become my husband.

I have always had a strong passion for all things health, wellbeing, fitness and fashion.

After I finished school, I studied for a Diploma of Fitness and worked at a bar in Geelong – which, to this day, is still one of my favourite jobs I've ever had!

After completing my Certificate IV, I stopped my study and moved to Sydney to be with my then boyfriend, not long after he had suffered a horrific football injury.

I got myself a casual job in a clothing store to meet people, planning to find my feet and continue my study. Instead, I stayed working there for six years. I met some of the most amazing people in that job, both colleagues and customers.

I got engaged in 2014 and married in 2016.

The following year, I fell pregnant. Little did I know how much of a journey I'd have ahead of me.

I found out I was pregnant at three weeks, found out I was having twins at seven weeks, and at eleven weeks found out that one of our babies had a neural tube defect known as anencephaly.

These babies are born with an underdeveloped brain and an incomplete skull.

These babies are not compatible with life.

The rest of the pregnancy was a wave of emotions.

Preparing to become a parent is a lot. Preparing to become a parent to twins is a lot. Preparing to become a parent to twins, then knowing you will have to welcome one baby and say goodbye to another one, all in one hit, is even harder.

Throw in all the complications we had along the way and the whole experience was a struggle of epic proportions.

It was heavy, and it still is heavy to this day.

On 12 April 2018, our beautiful baby girls were born.

Bella Rae and Willow Nevaeh.

Perfect in every way.

I'd never felt so much love in my life.

Willow was with us for five hours, and we spent the most perfect five hours with our darling little angel.

The first few months of Bella's life were such a blur.

Then we moved from Sydney down to the Victorian coast. That's when I probably first started to notice how much I was struggling with a mixture of post-traumatic stress disorder, perinatal anxiety and postnatal depression.

I put my hand up, though. I acknowledged what I was feeling and I got help. I went to my GP, who referred me to a psychologist – who I still see to this day.

In 2019, I fell pregnant with Sadie.

This, in turn, opened up a whole new web of fresh wounds that I hadn't known were there.

For the whole pregnancy, I was in a state of worry that something would go wrong. With every pain, every ache, I worried.

But something else was going wrong, right in front of my eyes, that I was completely unaware of.

Motherhood consumes you. It chews up the old you and spits out someone completely new. These words, spoken by the psychotherapist Esther Perel, could not be more true: 'Having a baby is a psychological revolution that changes our relationships to almost everything and everyone.'

Amen!

My marriage was failing and I was completely unaware of it, too busy in the day-to-day happenings of 'mum life' to notice the signs that, looking back now, were clearly there.

Also, when you're so consumed by grief like I was, you spend your days just surviving, trying to make it through the day and not be triggered by things around you.

In March 2020, two weeks into a lockdown during the worldwide pandemic, Sadie Rose was born.

I felt an overwhelming amount of joy the moment the doctor said, 'It's a girl.'

I said, under my breath: *Thank you, Willow. Thank you for giving Bella the little sister she longs for.*

Sadie's arrival brought a new wave of emotions. The memories of Willow came flooding back thick and fast. Being in lockdown while having to be the rock of the family was also something I struggled with quite a lot.

I noticed my now ex-husband was struggling too, so I took a step back from asking him for any help. I was trying to be as sympathetic as possible with the way he was choosing to deal with his grief. (Little did I know he had other things on his mind.)

Feeding Sadie was hard. She refused breastfeeding from about seven weeks, so I pumped and fed her breastmilk via bottle until she was four months old.

Along with all that came having to deal with multiple tantrums from Bella on the daily, all while being in lockdown at home. *Gah!*

At the end of June, my ex-husband went away for work. He was supposed to be away, at most, for thirty days or so.

Things were rocky in our relationship but never did I think they were so bad that I'd get a phone call from him that ended our marriage.

So, in the middle of 2020, I became a single parent.

The next few months were some of the lowest days of my life, even lower than when we had welcomed and said goodbye to Willow.

I was dealt another trauma on top of a trauma that I thought I had completely healed from. Except I hadn't healed. And, then and there, I realised I never truly will.

I once read something by the writer Lexi Behrndt, who said, 'As far as I can see, grief will never truly end. It may become softer over time, more gentle, and some days will feel sharp. But grief will last as long as love does – forever.'

Another grieving process had begun.

And in between all that, I showed up every day for my girls.

I never once was not there for them.

They brought out a strength in me I never knew I had.

In the thick of all this, someone said to me, 'Be the role model your girls will be proud of.' And that saying has stuck with me, with every decision I have made since then.

I want to be the best role model I can be for my children.

I want them to grow up knowing and seeing that I did everything I could in the shittest of circumstances.

I want them to grow up and say, 'I want to be just like my mum.'

My life these days is a world away from where I thought I'd be. I believed I'd never love again, and that no one would want to love me with my extra baggage (the best extra baggage ever, if I do say so myself).

But I've found love again.

I met my partner in 2022, and we had an instant connection. We've welcomed a new member to our family, Archibald, and the girls are just obsessed with their new baby brother.

Life is truly the best it's ever been.

I say this as a reminder to anyone out there feeling exactly that way right now: hold on to hope. I promise you that everything gets better in time.

Fall down nine times and get up ten, hey?

ELLIE LEMONS
On redefining co-parenting

As I write this piece, there is a three-month-old baby who's fallen asleep on his playmat and a brown bulldog at my feet, and my daughter is colouring in a picture at the coffee table before me. She asks me where her dad is, and I explain he is upstairs doing some work but will swim with her later, or he can help her with her homework. She scrunches her nose up at the latter.

It's funny; as I've been so deep in the postnatal trenches for the second time, I've forgotten to zoom out, and to really take note of the abundance of love and gratitude I have for my life, even though it is nothing like I could have ever imagined.

My children's father and I separated when our daughter (who is now almost eight) was seven months old. He did overnights from the get-go and has been financially supportive of me so I can be the mother I want to be. For this, I will be forever grateful.

I was twenty-four years old when I became a single mum. Although I was financially supported and had a co-parent who very much wanted to be involved as much as possible, I found myself grieving the white-picket-fence dream I had always envisioned for myself.

I call the next three years my intense, forced-growth period. When my children's father shared his vision of us being friends, I wanted in. But it's one thing to want it and another to actually be able to get it; I realise now how much growth I had to achieve to get to where we are now. I had never seen separated parents get along well and I had never stayed friends with an ex-partner, so I really had to grow up and trust him to lead us in the right direction.

I used the understanding that the relationship our daughter sees us have will be an anchor for her future relationships. I let this guide me when I wasn't sure what the right thing to do was, or when I doubted myself.

Together we continue to fight the narrative of separated parents being *against* one another. Like most people, we understand that in such situations, it is only ever the children who lose. Instead, we have decided to see ourselves as a team, to move through life's ebbs and flows respecting one another, supporting one another and making decisions based on what is best for the whole family unit.

This goal of ours – to be an ironclad team for our daughter – has meant that during the past seven years we have lived together and lived separately. We have moved interstate and, more recently, overseas to follow my children's father's career and dreams.

Over the years we discussed the idea of having another baby within our co-parenting dynamic. I've always known

I wanted to have another child and, after having such success co-parenting and feeling so supported as a mother, it seemed to make sense to have another one together. This year we welcomed our son into the world and had the privilege of watching our daughter become a big sister.

It would be wrong to say it has all been easy. Like any relationship, or any family, it takes work and dedication to the goal, and a fair amount of sacrifice and compromise from all involved. But the fruits of our labour are incredible. The home we provide for our children is solid, full of laughter and dance parties and very little sleep.

It's my hope that this little snippet of our lives can plant a seed of possibilities, showing what life after a separation, with children involved, can look like when handled with care. That someone flicking through these pages could begin to imagine something outside of the box – an alternate ending to their story that makes sense for them.

The biggest piece of advice I can give any other co-parents out there hoping to make it work is to have a shared vision. Where do you *all* want to be in five years? What does it look like? How can you *all* work together to get to a place where everyone's needs are met?

This is never where I saw my life headed, but I can proudly say that our two beautiful children and the family unit we have created is my favourite achievement yet!

KELLIE MOSES
On healing your soul

When I was younger, I married someone I felt so safe with. We grew up on the same street, went to high school together. It was so safe ... until it wasn't.

During my marriage, I lost my dad. It was earth-shattering. Dad was only sixty-seven, and it was a sudden shock that rocked my family. We were so close, and I was devastated.

A year later, I was pregnant. At my first scan, I remember hearing the words, 'I'm sorry. Your baby doesn't have a heartbeat.' I miscarried at eleven weeks.

The grief I felt was severe, compounded by the grief of losing Dad. Fast-forward a year, and not only had I lost Dad and my baby but I'd lost my marriage. Now I was single and traumatised, trying to recover from the past few years and the deep trauma of the divorce.

I remember lying alone at night, crying and praying that I would one day get to be a mother again. I was progressing rapidly in my career, but my heart and soul only wanted one thing – to have my womb full of life once more.

I met a new partner a year after my marriage ended, and six months later, I was pregnant, full of deep joy and gratitude. My pregnancy was beautiful but stressful. There was a deep knowing in my body that this relationship wasn't established enough to hold what was coming.

I couldn't stay in my job, and soon I found myself three months' pregnant and jobless. I hadn't done any inner work at that point and felt like my world, my career that I had given my soul to, and my identity were all stripped away from me. Then my partner's business collapsed, and his dad was diagnosed with cancer. At twenty-five weeks, my cervix shortened and I was put on bed rest. How would we provide for the baby?

When my beautiful son, Mason, was born, I was filled with deep unconditional love for him. Motherhood quite literally cracked me open. But my relationship with my partner ended, and I moved in with my mother, as a single mother with a four-month-old baby, no job, no partner, a bucketload of trauma and four hundred dollars to my name. I had postnatal depletion and anxiety, and felt completely broken.

My career was non-existent and I was completely lost. I clearly remember putting my son's clothes into my father's closet. Immense shame flooded my body. I felt like I was failing my son. I felt so judged by others.

My situation also deeply triggered my own mother. I remember crying on the floor in the shower at her house as she told me, 'You have lost your job. You have nothing. You and this little boy will never have anything and life is going to be really, really hard for you now.'

I stayed with Mum for almost a year. Mason and I co-slept in my teenage bedroom. He woke every two hours and although I had such deep love for him, I was exhausted and depleted. It wasn't the way I wanted to land in motherhood. But I was grateful to have the support of my mother and sister.

After a year, Mason and I moved into my own home. We had very little behind us. I was teaching two days a week, and I remember earning $1350 a fortnight – and the mortgage was $1250. I had help from family to buy the house, plus I had support from Mum and child support from my ex, and was receiving Centrelink benefit payments. Mum had to buy us a washing machine when ours broke. I was trying to keep it together and be positive, but life felt exhausting. I was losing myself, and wasn't the mother I wanted to be. My ex saw Mason on Saturdays and would help during the week, but my biggest concern was Mason having two homes. We agreed that I would have him with me full time.

I was deep in my trauma and grief, and stuck in survival mode, with my anxiety at an all-time high. It felt like I was drowning. Slowly I started to realise that I was the only person who could change this situation for us, and that being stuck in this victim archetype wasn't serving me.

When Mason was almost two years old, I broke my arm and hit my absolute rock bottom. So I started focusing on healing physically and emotionally. I went through the spiral (a journey that helps you to let go), and let go of so many stories and so much subconscious patterning. I started to realise that my power was in the way I chose to respond to things, and that I am the powerful creator of my reality. *I* get to create our story. What had happened was done and I couldn't change it, but I could change the trajectory of the future reality for my son and me.

I started choosing me, and focusing on the things that brought me joy. In choosing me, I was choosing Mason. I learned how to protect and clear my energy and how to set boundaries, and I slowly started to come back into my power. I started to become grateful for the setbacks and decided that instead of drowning in sorrow and grief, I would use them as a power to help me shift forward. I learned about death and rebirth and alchemy.

I started focusing on what I *did* have: the abundance, love, support and family around us, and the most divine little soul who I had waited thirty-four years for. I started healing. I stopped numbing and drinking too much. I went through the spiral again and in 2020 I took a huge leap of faith and started a business to create what I had needed.

I didn't want any woman or mother to ever feel like I had felt and not have the emotional support she needed. There had been nowhere for me to go: psychologists were booked out for six months in advance and I'd needed support. I'd needed a safe, non-judgemental space and community where I didn't feel alone. So I created it.

I continued to do the inner work and deconstruct my limiting beliefs. I became fiercely dedicated to my healing journey, to coming out of my hyper-independent masculine energy, and to regulating regulate my nervous system and slowing down. I learned to embody my nurturing feminine energy and created a beautiful, safe, loving, peaceful home for Mason and me.

Today, I am overflowing with gratitude and love. I have learned to love and accept myself, and am so grateful that I am able to emotionally support so many women and children. I have the most divine, soulful, beautiful boy who fills me with complete love and joy every single day. I adore him and, to be honest, I wouldn't change a thing. I love our life and I can sit back now and see how some things needed to collapse to create space for what was coming. In many ways, my son aligned me with my soul's purpose. His birth collapsed everything that wasn't in alignment with my highest purpose, even though it felt like a dark night of the soul at the time.

If you are in the trenches and are reading this, look after yourself. Take time every single day to pour into you. In choosing you, you are choosing your children. You have a limited amount of emotional energy each day and it's not selfish to set boundaries and fill up our own cups first. You can't be a present, giving, nurturing mother if you are depleted. Make space to do the inner work. It's a gift to you and to your children. Perception is projection, and your internal world creates your external world.

You have your whole life ahead of you.
You are worthy.
You are enough.
You are lovable.
Your children need you to be happy and full of joy.
Take the space to find you again.
She is there, ready for you.
Healing is messy and beautiful.
You are exactly where you need to be.
And your beautiful children chose *you*.
Hold your head high and walk through the fire.
You are an alchemist.
You will rise from this.
I promise.

EMILY MCKAY
On the hardest decisions

I always knew I wanted to be a mum. Not in the sense that it was to be my sole purpose in life, but I always had a feeling deep down and a belief that one day it would happen, when the time was right.

The first time I thought I was going to parent on my own wasn't when I separated from my partner. It was when I was standing on top of the Bolte Bridge, newly pregnant. I will never forget that feeling. It will be ingrained in me forever. The abandoned car. The person I was searching for nowhere in sight.

Two police officers had arrived just before me. I don't know what I said or did in those minutes from when I arrived on the bridge to when I was put into the back of a police car. All I knew was that I was looking for the father of my unborn child, and he was gone.

The drive from the bridge to the hospital was the longest ten minutes of my life. I sat in the back of the car numb, scared, pregnant and alone, with no answers. Until the first update came in: someone had been retrieved from beneath the bridge. Then the second update: he was alive.

After that night, the months of my partner's recovery were long and hard. Physically and mentally, nothing could have prepared me for what was to come.

Having miscarried only months before, I thought my chances of it happening again were incredibly high. How could my body go through this much shock, stress and trauma and still be able to carry a pregnancy to term? But, by some miracle, it did.

Physically, my pregnancy was a breeze. I was lucky enough to enjoy every milestone and cherish every special connection that could be felt along the way. That was what gave me the strength and belief to get through those challenging times.

After nine long months of pregnancy, I almost gave birth in the emergency waiting room. It was a busy night at the Royal Women's Hospital and every birthing suite was full. After hours of labouring in the emergency room, we were finally taken upstairs to our room. I couldn't hold back the urge to push and, what felt like moments later, our beautiful baby boy was born. We hadn't found out the baby's sex beforehand, so the surprise made it all the more special. I was in a total state of bliss. All my dreams of being a mum had come true.

The second time I thought I would parent on my own was when I made that choice. Hendrix was six months old when I officially separated from his dad. Over those six months, there had been so many happy times that I will never forget. The joy and the feeling of being in a love bubble with a newborn were incredible. But most of those happy times were only with me and Hendrix. The awareness that I was parenting alone had started to sink in.

Deciding to separate was not easy: not a split-second decision, but one that I had thought long and hard about. A decision that had to be made, *needed* to be made. For me, but mostly – and most importantly – for my son.

Sometimes we need to make choices that put us back into a place where we have control. As many single mothers know, you don't make these decisions lightly. You try and you try and you try until something changes in *you*. For me, the biggest change was watching my son grow up and seeing him take in all the information around him. Seeing him become aware. A time comes when you realise: *They know what's happening*. Maybe not every intricate detail, but the big parts: who is there for them, who is showing up, what people say and do to show their love. And as his mother, I made the decision to put him first, ahead of everything and everyone.

Taking that step to go out on your own can be so scary. You'll ask yourself: *Am I doing the right thing? Can I actually do this? Have I tried hard enough for my child? Am I going to be enough?*

But the truth is, I knew I could do it long before the decision was made. Facing the truths of *I can do this* and *I need to do this* came to me at different times. Looking back, I'm proud of myself for walking away when I did. Yes, it was (effing) hard. Yes, I had a hell of a lot of support from family and friends. And yes, I cried for days, possibly weeks. But at the same time, I had an overwhelming feeling that I was making the right decision for everyone involved.

Raising my son on my own is incredibly rewarding. Right now, five years on, I'm his whole world. I'm his anchor. I'm proud of myself for the life we have. I work hard to make sure he feels safe, loved and secure. Knowing I give that to him fills me with happiness every single day.

ZOE GEORGE
On finding your confidence

I grew up in a very strict household, which meant no boyfriends until I was eighteen. I never really thought about marriage until, at the ripe old age of twenty-nine, I started panicking when I found myself suddenly single. For a Greek girl, being unmarried at thirty meant you were essentially 'on the shelf'.

I met my husband after only four months of being single and decided to navigate this relationship quite differently. On paper, he seemed the right choice.

Are your parents still married? was one of the first things I asked him, almost instinctively. In my Greek culture, divorce felt like a taboo – a failure that brought dishonour to your parents, because quite often they cared more about what others would say than their child's happiness. My parents were still (un)happily together, like many other couples of their generation, and I guess I just expected my life would be the same. Divorce was never an option for me or my partner.

I thought if I found someone with a similar upbringing, we'd both have a clear path to follow, a blueprint for our future.

For years, we had a great life. We were the couple all our friends envied because we were always laughing and having fun. We were best friends, and trusted each other completely in all aspects of our lives. Having kids completed that picture-perfect image of what I'd written about in my diary as a young girl. Don't get me wrong – there were some tiny hiccups in the beginning. But bigger problems were brewing under the surface that would bring my perfect world to an end.

It wasn't an easy decision to end our marriage, but eventually it became painfully clear that we'd given it way too many chances. Things were too far gone. Yet the thought of becoming a single mother terrified me. I never doubted my abilities as a mother, but the impending change loomed large. I worried constantly about whether I would manage everything on my own, even little things like switching utility companies, the banking, the lawns, the things he had been responsible for. He helped around the house, though I had always felt like I had done the most and needed a second me. It's one thing to feel like you're doing everything, but it's another to *actually* do everything.

Ending the marriage also meant relinquishing control. My husband and I shared similar values in parenting, a cohesion I had cherished. But the prospect of separation stirred fears of what could change. What if he found someone new, someone who would influence our children's lives in ways I couldn't predict, or ways I didn't like? The unknown was daunting, an undercurrent of anxiety that pulled at me with every passing day. Many, many times I considered 'staying for the kids', as many do.

Finances weighed heavily on my mind too. Like many single mothers, I feared the implications of supporting my family alone. Would I be able to give them the life they'd grown accustomed to? As a sole trader, my income fluctuated unpredictably, which was so scary for me. I'm the type of person who needs financial security. I need to know what five years ahead looks like. Taking on a mortgage by myself felt impossible, yet I desperately wanted to keep our home, to preserve some semblance of normalcy for the kids. I was determined to minimise the upheaval in their lives.

Growing up, I had been taught that unless there was infidelity or abuse, you simply didn't leave a marriage. The man I married had neither cheated nor laid a hand on me, so I hung in there, some might say longer than I should have. I kept giving the marriage extra chances, hoping for change, but as time went by the disconnect became greater and new issues began to arise. I realised something had to give.

I used to tell people about what it felt like at the time: as if I was in a boat with my family, and my relationship was a drill that was constantly drilling holes into the bottom of the boat. I was scooping out the water and blocking up those holes as well as trying to paddle to get my family to safety. But once I pushed that relationship overboard, blocked up the holes, cut off the anchor that was slowing us down and kept paddling with me and my kids, it actually felt like I was no longer sinking. I was now able to paddle forward smoothly.

When the papers were signed and the weight of indecision lifted, I was surprised by how liberated I felt. I must admit, it helped that our separation had been so amicable at that stage. I entered a new routine, one that felt like I had finally reclaimed my life. I embraced the healing journey, recognising that this was my choice. I chose to focus on myself and the children – no dating, not for a long time. I realised there were people out there who had my back and supported me without question. For the first time in years, I felt empowered, like a boss, handling everything with grace, *on my own*.

My children were thriving, and I was meeting my financial obligations. I hadn't asked anyone for help. Each day was productive; I was actively building a life I loved. I planned a trip to Europe for us, a reward for the tough years we had gotten through. I'd never looked at my new situation and cried, 'Woe is me.' I saw the positives of being on my own. Loneliness was not my companion; I had a solid group of friends and a supportive network that made life feel vibrant again. I even feel like I look the best I have in years because beauty really does shine from within, and my energy is just different now.

My ex-husband and I established a workable co-parenting arrangement. We wanted the kids to have stability, and we agreed that would mean them waking up in the same home during the school week and not being burdened by transitions. We navigated our new reality with flexibility. Our door was always open to him. He started coming over for dinners and engaging with the kids, and we saw the joy it brought them. This new dynamic felt healthy, and I was determined to maintain it. I'm not sure if it will always be this way but for now, I feel blessed that we can be 'friends' for the kids.

There was power in letting go of the anger I could have clung to. Instead of allowing resentment to fester over finances or perceived slights, I focused on my own mental health. I learned to take the higher road. I recognised that staying angry would only drain my energy and distract from the life I was building.

Professionally, I began to value myself more. After stepping back due to my parents' health issues, I returned to my work with a renewed sense of purpose. Encouraged by friends and mentors, I raised my prices and reduced my workload, striking a balance that allowed me to enjoy both my professional and personal lives.

I had taken time to rediscover every aspect of my worth, and I was no longer searching for someone to complete me; I was whole on my own. My experiences had shown me the value of self-awareness, and I refused to settle for anything less than someone who matched my energy and aspirations.

As I navigated this new chapter, I reflected on the lessons I had learned. I understood the importance of watering my own grass before seeking out new lawns. We didn't end our marriage out of boredom or desire for something better; I feel as though it was the best decision for myself and my children. My ex was a good man, and I hope that our children will see our commitment to maintaining a respectful relationship. As the saying goes: don't be sad that it ended, but happy that it happened.

I'm so grateful to have my two blessings, and he was a good choice as the father of my children, irrespective of whether we could make it work or not. The truth is that I soon realised I was thriving in my independence. I am no longer waiting for someone else to step in and make things better. I am proud of the life I am creating – one filled with love, resilience and the promise of new beginnings. I have taken the right course and paddled forward, determined to make the most of this second chance. And I know, above all, that we will be just fine.

GRETA BRIDGETTE
On life on the other side

Ever since I can remember, I have always yearned to be a mother. That may have come from some absences I felt between me and my mother; it may have been a maternal instinct; or I may have felt so lonely in this world on my own that I thought being a mum would make me feel whole.

I grew up in the small coastal town of Byron Bay in New South Wales. I was in a relationship from the age of twenty-one with a man who would eventually be my fiancé. We were together for fourteen years and I was happy, thinking I'd found my forever. He was tall, dark and tattooed, with muscles in all the right places but not too bulked up. Am I painting the picture correctly?

He was my rock and understood things about me that made me feel safe. That all changed.

I fell pregnant with our first baby at thirty-two. I still remember Aunt Flo being late (and she was never late), so I took a pregnancy test. It showed two dark lines. Positive.

At the time, I lived on my family's property, and we had all just moved from town to a farm nearby. I was there alone – well alone, with 40 hectares of property and all of my thoughts and overwhelmed emotions.

I showed the test to my sister-in-law, who is now my best friend, and asked her, 'Am I pregnant?'

She said, 'Yep, you sure bloody are!'

Then I remember trying to hide it in the dirt beside our house so that my mum and brother wouldn't find the positive test. I was scared of how they would react when they found out, and worried what they would think of me. By then, my relationship with my partner wasn't great, but I thought it might get better. I'd had a miscarriage before, and I wanted to have a baby so badly.

Fast-forward ten months and I was living in an apartment on the Gold Coast with my partner – he had become my fiancé – and our son. There were red flags in my relationship that I ignored. Was it ignorance or a deliberate denial? I'm not sure. I think both.

Fast-forward another year and I fell pregnant again, then miscarried.

When Covid came to visit the world, we had just bought a little duplex on the Gold Coast. My son was now one and I remember thinking that our lives were going to get better. *Everything will be better – my relationship, my finances, my mental health.*

However, things got worse.

Six months went by, and I was pregnant again. Despite our problems, I remember being so grateful. I couldn't believe I was pregnant – another chance at a family, a sibling for our son. *How lucky are we?*

It was through my second pregnancy, as I cried myself to sleep with my son koala-gripping me, that I decided I'd had enough. I could see the flags so clearly. I sat with these feelings for a long time and weighed up my options. Could I do this solo?

At the time, it was a terrifying thought. I was twenty weeks pregnant and had an almost-two-year-old, but I've never been more set on anything in my entire life. My mind was made up. *I'm leaving.* No matter how difficult single parenting would be, I was sure that what I was enduring each day was worse. So I put my wedding ring on my other hand and I left.

I gave birth to my beautiful daughter, a fiery redhead with a personality to match. Strong, resilient and independent. That evening will be embedded in my scattered mind forever. My mother and sister-in-law were present. I'll never stop thanking them for guiding me when I needed it most.

I remember bawling through contractions. I couldn't stop myself feeling alone. *Why do I have to do this with no partner by my side?* I felt worthless.

Then it was me, my new home, a newborn and my two-year-old son. And the silence that comes with being alone. Not alone for an hour or so. Like, *alone* alone. I had support from my mum and family, but some days that support didn't feel like enough. I remember questioning if I had postnatal depression because I felt so emotional and moody almost all the time.

Maybe I was angry that I had got myself in this situation, or it could have been from the string of pharmaceutical drugs I was taking for an infection from my C-section wound. I felt hurt and ashamed for a while. I also felt strength, power and resilience after what I had finally done.

Deciding to be a single parent is never easy.

Navigating a break-up through Covid when my family was on the other side of the border and trying to be present for my little humans were some of the most difficult things I will ever endure. But there was also a sense of ease, safety and extreme happiness. I had my babies, and I had a home filled with love and happiness. We didn't (we *don't*) have a lot, but we have one another and that is a gift I'll never take for granted.

Sure, there are moments when I get lonely and I would love someone to share my day with, to cuddle on the couch with, or to help me with the mental and physical load of parenting, but nothing beats your internal happiness and that sense of certainty.

Co-parenting is tough. *Bloody tough.* It took us years to get to where we are. Some days it works wonderfully; other days I want to scratch his and my eyes out. But as a mother whose path hasn't been easy, my one true belief is that no matter what's happened or what's going to happen, as long as you and your children are safe and feel loved, that's the best thing you can give them.

I work two to three days a week, juggling a nine-to-five job, then I pick up the kids from daycare.

I find it hard prioritising play and household duties as it's just me. Like, *Yes, I'd love to come and play Lego with you but just right now I'm in the middle of cooking dinner because if I don't who will?*

I do everything. I even do the lawns. I get burnt out and my brain never stops ticking. There are one billion tabs open, even when I place my head on my pillowcase, which most likely needs a wash. I wouldn't swap it for anything, though. Okay, maybe a maid and chef.

I'm proud of how far I've come in my journey. I still have a long way to go.

But as long as my children feel loved and safe, I know I've done my job. I love being their mumma. I'd move mountains to make them happy and keep them safe.

They're my best friends *forever*.

(We say that every night to each other, all snuggled up in my king-size bed.)

ANONYMOUS
On surviving with strength

I was thirty-one when I met my ex-partner. He was thirty-three and had two children from a previous relationship. I had been single for about five years, enjoying my independence. But when I met him, everything changed. He called me the day after we met at a festival, a gesture I loved because it showed his confidence. We started dating, doing everything together, from dining out to attending car boot sales.

I had a rule against dating men with children, but he made me rethink that. His kids were young, and I was introduced to them gradually. We spent every weekend together, and soon enough, he moved into my three-bedroom apartment. We were deeply in love, and within the first few months, I said, 'I love you.' We knew we were meant to be together.

Our life was a mix of family time and social outings. We travelled overseas, and our bond grew stronger. After a year together, he proposed in a grand gesture involving a speedboat and a picnic on a secluded beach. It was a magical *yes*.

We had a beautiful wedding, a small and elegant affair. After the wedding, we bought a house and set up our own businesses. Life was perfect, and soon we started talking about having a child of our own. It took us about two years to conceive, but the wait was worth it. My pregnancy was easy, and I embraced my role as a mum-to-be with enthusiasm.

However, the pregnancy brought changes. Our social life took a back seat, and my partner seemed different. He wasn't the happy, funny guy I'd married. He became angry and unmotivated. While my business thrived, his struggled, and he spent many days lying on the couch. I thought these were normal relationship bumps that would smooth out once the baby arrived.

But things only got worse after our daughter was born. He became increasingly angry and distant. Two days after I came home from the hospital, he went out with friends to celebrate, leaving me alone with the baby. His parents had to stay with me while he was out drinking. He returned to work quickly, leaving me without the support I needed.

Three weeks after our daughter was born, I called his mum, suspecting something was seriously wrong. His behaviour became erratic, and our once-happy life started to crumble. I thought he might be having an affair or using drugs. My suspicions weren't unfounded; he had an addictive personality. He had struggled with overeating, smoking and drinking in the past.

In the end, the love that once seemed unbreakable was tested by life's challenges. Our story, which had begun with love hearts and grand gestures, became a tale of struggle and heartbreak. But through it all, I held on to the memories of our beautiful moments, hoping for a brighter future.

I knew he had an all-or-nothing personality. But nothing could have ever prepared me for the discovery that would shatter our family. His eldest daughter found him smoking something out of a pipe. When confronted, he admitted to smoking crack but promised it was a one-off. I believed him at first, thinking the issue would now be behind us.

However, red flags started appearing everywhere. I found a pipe on the couch, and his excuses grew more elaborate. He'd say he'd been to the park with the dog, but the dog wasn't tired. Money started disappearing, along with the kids' musical instruments. A holiday to Bali was a disaster; he became aggressive and rude and spent all day in bed. It was at this point I started to realise that I was dealing with a severe problem and began digging for information. I soon learned that he was using ice, not crack. Despite his lies and the turmoil, I still loved him and wanted to help him stop. We went to counselling, where he admitted to using ice sporadically but claimed he didn't have a problem.

Desperate to connect with him, I agreed to try methamphetamine with him one night while our daughter was with her grandmother. The experience was powerful and for the first time in a long time, we felt connected again. But I refused to do it again.

Despite all my efforts, he continued using and deteriorating further. He lost his job, and his life spiralled out of control.

I sat him down one day and explained the consequences of his addiction: he would lose his children, his job and his family. He promised to stop, but his words were empty. His addiction worsened, leading to more fights and even the heartbreaking discovery that he had been with sex workers. Despite everything, I still stood by him, hoping for a breakthrough.

Finally, with no job, no money and nowhere else to turn, he agreed to go to rehab. It was a last-ditch effort to save our family and his life, and I desperately hoped it would be enough to bring back the man I loved and secure a future for our child.

However, it wasn't long after his release from rehab that the lies resumed. He would often claim he was going to the store but return with red eyes, having clearly used drugs again. He constantly dismissed my concerns, calling me a psycho and refusing to discuss the issue. Despite all my growing doubts and his manipulation, I clung to the man I had loved before drugs took hold of him.

We decided to sell our beautiful home to alleviate financial stress and moved into a rental with more space for our children. But he squandered his share of the profits on drugs, sex workers and a jet ski. Rock bottom truly came when I found my one-year-old daughter holding an ice pipe.

Confronted with this dangerous reality, I knew that I had to leave.

With my young daughter in tow, I moved out and secured a new apartment. Although leaving him was heart-wrenching, I knew that I needed to prioritise my daughter's safety. Despite the darkness and shattered dreams, my decision to leave was driven by an unwavering commitment to protect my daughter.

My ex-husband, now left to his own devices, sank deeper into his addiction. I tried to detach emotionally but continued to assist him with fuel and food while avoiding giving him money. Yet none of it helped. His life deteriorated even further, leading to him being evicted from his home and living in his car. At one point he went missing, and I feared the worst.

His addiction to ice had gradually consumed all of our lives, leaving me in a constant state of turmoil. The emotional toll eventually became too much, plunging me into depression.

Friends and family rallied around me offering their support, but it wasn't enough to fill the void. My life felt empty and nothing seemed to bring me joy anymore. I turned to antidepressants to cope, which allowed me to maintain some semblance of normalcy for my daughter. Weeks turned into months, with my ex drifting in and out of my life. Occasionally, he would call from a phone box, having sold his phone for drugs.

It was around this time I decided to buy an apartment, as a fresh start. My ex had offered his help during this time and yet I soon found myself heartbroken again; his true intention had been to gain access to my new home and steal from me once again. This betrayal was the final straw.

It's been many years since then and I haven't spoken to him in all that time. He left our family to chase an addiction and hasn't contacted us. I've had to rebuild my life from the ground up, focusing on providing a stable and loving environment for my child. It's painful to think her father might be doing well without us. Explaining it to our inquisitive daughter is tough. She asks about her daddy, and I have to say he got sick. It's easier to say that than he turned into a bad man, but I assure her that he loves her and thinks of her daily.

In 2022, I wasn't feeling well despite staying active and running my business. After ten months, I was diagnosed with terminal lung cancer – at thirty-nine, and as a non-smoker. The cancer had metastasised to my lymph nodes, liver, spine, pelvis and shoulders. I was given six months to live without treatment and possibly eighteen months with treatment.

I refused to accept this fate and sought treatment overseas, achieving fantastic results. Now I'm cancer-free.

It's hard to imagine that the darkest time in my life was losing my husband to drug addiction, not terminal cancer. I had no control over his actions, but I felt like I had some control over my cancer. I fought hard to survive for my daughter. The drug addiction took away much more than the disease. It took my husband, my best friend and my daughter's daddy. The fight against cancer made me stronger and showed me how powerful I could be. It gave me more than it took away. If it weren't for my daughter, I might have accepted my fate. But she didn't have a dad and so I refused to let the cancer take her mum away from her too.

I often reflect on the happy times with him – the times he made me laugh, our engagement, and the beauty of our wedding. Those memories are precious to me, even though I would hardly recognise the man he is today. Focusing on those good moments helps me stay positive.

Life is good for me right now. Everything seems to be heading in the right direction. I am happy and I am healthy. I've spent some time in the dating pool but haven't found anyone special yet. When I choose a man, it will be for the long term. I want someone who will accept both me and my daughter.

She often asks about getting a daddy – questions like, 'When I get a daddy, can he come camping with us? Where will he sleep?' It makes us giggle, but it also speaks to the void she feels. It's challenging to find the right person who ticks all the boxes. But I'm ready to fall in love again, with someone who will not only be a partner to me but a positive male figure for her. I'll wait until the right one comes along.

MOTHERING ON OUR OWN

HIND AL-AZZAM
On becoming a teen mum

I had a challenging childhood. My parents separated when I was just two years old. My dad, a devout Muslim, raised me in a very conservative household. Growing up, I had to cover up from head to toe, I wasn't allowed to wear make-up, and talking to boys was out of the question.

My mum, on the other hand, battled anxiety and depression. By the time I was four, my brothers and I were in foster care as she navigated her mental health struggles. Thankfully, she got better, and after a year we were reunited. It wasn't a typical childhood, but I had a great experience in foster care and remain connected to the family that took care of us.

I met my ex-boyfriend at primary school. He was my first crush, and our bond only grew stronger when we ended up in the same high school. By the end of Year 8, our crush had evolved into a more serious relationship. Reflecting back, I realise how young and immature we both were, clueless about what lay ahead.

I remember the moment I found out I was pregnant as vividly as if it happened yesterday. My period was only two days late, but I had this gut feeling. I confided in my mum, and I took a pregnancy test. I'll never forget walking out of the bathroom to tell her the test was positive. Despite my fears, she was nothing but supportive. I was only fourteen, but with my mother by my side, I knew everything would be okay.

At her suggestion, I waited a few days before telling my boyfriend. Then impatience got the better of me, and I went to his house to share the news. He was lying on his bed when I told him. He rolled over and faced the wall, a reaction that foreshadowed the challenges to come.

We kept the news to ourselves for weeks. The confirmation came from a blood test, but soon after that my boyfriend's mum found out. She was furious, and it was clear her family did not want me to have the baby. I understood her fear for her son, but being banned from their house and told that this would ruin his life was a harsh blow.

Eventually, both families met to discuss the situation. In the eyes of my boyfriend's family, abortion was the only option. But my mum stood by me, making it clear she would support whatever decision I made.

You might wonder if I considered an abortion. At fourteen, the thought didn't even cross my mind. I had an unshakable belief that everything would be okay. With my mum's support, I could do it. However, as tensions rose with my boyfriend's family, doubts began to creep in. Briefly, I wondered if I was mentally prepared to raise a child. But I overcame those fears, especially when his family said they didn't want him taking any responsibility.

I knew then this would be my journey alone.

Despite everything, I stayed in school throughout my pregnancy. My mum was incredible, rallying support from social services and connecting me with a young mums program. I walked around school with my head held high, proud of my pregnancy and indifferent to any judgement. Sometimes I felt self-conscious in public, but overall, I owned my pregnant belly.

I didn't have a detailed birth plan, and my labour turned out to be traumatic. Jordan wasn't breathing when he was born. They rushed him to the table to resuscitate him. I was under a spinal block, feeling like I was on another planet. The relief when he started breathing was indescribable. The moment they placed him on my chest, I fell in love instantly.

My mum took time off work to help me during the first few weeks. We operated like shiftworkers, taking turns for every wake. I was exhausted, but infinitely grateful for my mum's support as I soaked up every moment with my tiny new love.

I knew my school friendships would change once Jordan was born. It's been hard to stay connected. One of my close friends often tells me I've changed so much. It's difficult to explain that I *am* different now – I am a mum. I'm back at school now, thanks to a program for young mums. There are about six of us, and we attend four days a week, bringing our children along. A child educator watches them while we study. It's challenging, especially with a clingy child, but I'm determined to finish Years 11 and 12.

My plan is to become a midwife. Despite the trauma of my labour, I remember one incredibly kind midwife who made a difference. I want to be that person for other mothers. Like most sixteen-year-olds, I'm on social media. It can be tough watching girls my age live their lives, but I know I'll have my time. I've started going to the gym every night when Jordan is asleep, finding happiness in that routine.

I have so many hopes and dreams for our future. I want to finish Year 12, study midwifery, and one day settle down, have more kids and be with someone who loves us both. My family struggled financially when I was growing up, and I hope to provide a better life for Jordan.

Jordan has the best little personality. He looks so much like my mum and is just as funny. He can't talk yet, just gibberish, but it's the kind of gibberish only a mother can understand.

I've told my mum that whatever happens, I'm never leaving. If I move out, she's coming with me.

One of the biggest heartbreaks has been losing my relationship with my father because of my pregnancy. We haven't spoken since he found out. It feels like I'm a disappointment to him. I haven't heard from Jordan's dad either. His family moved away and cut all contact. It's heartbreaking, feeling unloved.

Every night, I dream about my dad and Jordan's dad. I dream that one day they might choose to come back into our lives. But even if they don't, I feel sad for them. They're missing out on the most beautiful little boy. And I'm going to enjoy the best life, with or without them.

MOTHERING ON OUR OWN

MICHELLE RYAN
On choosing happiness

The beginning / broken

For an entire week, it felt as though my whole wide world had crashed down around me. I couldn't fathom or comprehend how on earth I would ever feel happiness again.

I remember feeling the most terrified at the thought of going from full-time mum to having to share my darling boy, Jiah, for the rest of his upbringing. What might be only a few days each week would turn into weeks, then months, and ultimately I would lose years of my life with him. I didn't become a mother to only parent part time, and I wasn't sure my heart would ever accept this.

I pulled myself out of bed in the mornings because I had to show up for my boy. I painted a smile on my face and switched off my pain in his presence because the last thing that I wanted was for this separation to impact him or bring him sadness too. The rubble that surrounded me all seemed just too much to rummage through. There was so much noise in my head, and I'd crumble the moment I was left alone.

I remember reading a quote that said, 'Happiness is a choice. You cannot choose what happens to you, but you can choose the life you want to live.' This quote landed powerfully for me – so much so that I made a promise to myself to wake up every day making choices for my future happy life, not for my past.

The middle / sticky survival

After the initial shock and sadness, I went into survival mode, and this is what saved me. When it was a 'just me' day, I surrounded myself with people I love and trust. I cried, I talked, they tried to feed me. I moved my body, soaked up fresh air, kept on top of to-do lists, kept on top of work and, most importantly, started to map out a new future for myself and my son.

When someone you have adored and trusted for ten years (or any amount of time) breaks this trust, you very quickly realise that you need to now make decisions for you and your child only. Nothing else matters.

I struggled to shift my default mindset from making decisions as a devoted wife to making them as a solo mother. It was something that I needed to consciously remind myself to do.

It's just you now, babe, I'd repeat to myself daily.

The sticky days for me were the hardest. Trying to communicate with someone who now feels like a stranger. Detangling myself from not only a marriage but a completely intertwined life. The logistics of living situations, custody arrangements, financials, shared businesses and possessions, negotiations, disagreements, agreeing on something, disagreeing again. I felt constantly unsettled by the unknown, a million and one thoughts running through my head at night while in limbo, not knowing what lay ahead.

I couldn't sleep.

I felt too sick to eat.

'One day at a time,' everyone around me would say. But I didn't want to take it one day at a time. I wanted to close my eyes and wake up twelve months into the future. I wanted to skip the messiness and the hard work. But sometimes what you want and what you're dealing with in life are two very, very different matters. So you do what you have to do to push through, to move forward. And those messy, heavy, dark days are the days I found strength that I didn't even know I had. And for that, I'm now grateful.

I turned my pain into power, 'one day at a time'. I showed myself that I was braver and stronger than I'd ever believed or realised I could be. This has reshaped me as a person. The moment I shifted my perspective to healing and new beginnings was when I started to truly feel like myself again. You can spend years of your life dwelling on what went wrong and why, but will that change the now and your future? *Definitely not.*

Once I started to emotionally heal, I started to realise that this new era of my life was something that I wanted to embrace and make the very most of.

The now / thriving

As the days, weeks and months passed, I started to feel lighter and brighter than I ever had before. As I reflected on my ten-year relationship, I truly made peace with the fact that my ex-partner was not my forever person. I'm a self-confessed hopeless romantic, and when I look back on the past, I think that some days I truly convinced myself that I was happier than I was. I thought if I *believed* I was happy, I would be happy. I can tell you now, that's not how it works out.

Yes, I now have a little less time with my boy, but the quality of this time is so much better. I have never been a more present mother, and I am so proud of that. There are now two very distinct versions of myself:

Version 1: Just me. I work my butt off to support my son, and spend my extra time filling *my* cup and no one else's! I spend time with my family, go to Pilates every single day, listen to my favourite music up loud, enjoy a late-night wine with my best friends. I sleep in if my body tells me to. I read, meditate, soak up the sun, have a bath, light a candle, go for long walks and re-energise my soul, so that when it's time for me to re-enter my mother version I am the 100 per cent best version I can be.

Allowing myself to flow and explore this new version of myself has been liberating and empowering, and my daily smiles are no longer painted on.

Version 2: Mother. This will forever be my favourite version of myself, for the rest of my life.

'It'll all make sense one day,' I told myself daily. And it already does.

मोTHERING ON OUR OWN

EMMA JUNE
On acceptance fatigue

My friend asks me how I'm going. We're in a coffee shop in my small town and I'm searching for a response to her question that won't alarm any of the five children (three mine, two hers) that are half-busy, half-bored around us. Although she isn't asking about anything in particular, my brain, still, only knows how to answer in relation to that thing that happened.

'I have acceptance fatigue,' I respond, deflated.

She knows what I mean. She is a good friend. Not in the sense that we've known each other for a long time or see each other every week, but in the sense that she's good for me. She gets me. She, like me, knows grief, having lost her family home in the catastrophic floods in the New South Wales Northern Rivers in 2022.

'Acceptance fatigue.'

We contemplate this together for a moment. It's the first time I've used this expression to describe how I'm feeling. *Acceptance fatigue*: to be tired of accepting. To be tired of 'being the bigger person', of 'taking the high road', of responding 'graciously'. It's another layer of the tiredness we experience as mothers.

My friend's nod and downward glance hint that she too is fatigued by the impossible task of accepting the unacceptable. Her unacceptable: a natural disaster that robbed her, her husband and their children of their home. Mine: a betrayal that robbed me and my children of a family. And robbed me of my dignity and access to choice.

When I sit with my friend in the coffee shop it is twenty-something months since D-Day, and eighteen months since I began living alone in the family home with my children, mine only half the time. I am somehow simultaneously unrecognisable yet more myself than ever. I am broken but stronger, lost but smarter, fearful but calm, a co-parent but an ex-wife, burning but cool water. Over the past almost two years I have had more emotions flow through me than they dare to put on the pie charts in our children's classrooms. I've spiralled and I've soared, and where I have landed today, this day that I am drinking coffee, enveloped in the safety of friendship and sisterhood, is *tired*. Of all of it. This fatigue isn't like the newborn days, which are hard but full of purpose and life. Instead, it is absolutely senseless. I am so tired because I still just can't make sense of what happened to my life.

My story of becoming a single woman and a single mum is one of betrayal. And then of rejection, fear, depression and grief, woven, eventually, with a delicate thread of healing, family and daring to trust again. I am still very defined but what happened. I was content in my marriage. My marriage wasn't bad. Until I discovered it was.

When I describe my marriage and the discovery to my (third) therapist for the first time, I give her the house analogy.

'It's like my marriage was a house with cracks. And instead of tending to the cracks or even acknowledging their presence, for fear of how much work it would be fix them (what if they are irreparable?), all our attention went to the facade of the house. Street appeal. How it all looked to the outside world. And then,' I exclaim to my therapist, because I am chuffed I have it all so figured out, 'a *bomb* went off and the house collapsed.' Then I reassure her: 'But it's okay, because now we get to start again and rebuild something stronger, with a better foundation.'

She nods along. She gets it.

'But I realised that, while I wanted to pick through the rubble of my house and examine the importance and sentimentality of what remained, he wanted to toss the lot and move somewhere else. He couldn't stand to look at our mess.'

It took me three months of standing before the rubble, in a state of shock, to realise that if I wanted to stay here and address the brokenness, I'd best do it alone.

The twenty-something months that have passed have untangled me from him a little, but not enough. It is the great tragedy of divorce with children that you part ways but are never fully apart (unless, of course, there is the devastation of the absent co-parent). It is as though my separation has been the sun and around it revolves the rest of my life: my thoughts and relationships and parenting and identity. It is my defining feature. 'Single mum' takes centrestage and I, Emma, am her shadow.

The senseless and relentless not-knowing, the striving to accept and to heal, the trudge through grief, the practice of grace, the hope for the future, the trying not to implode, the nurturing of the children through it all, the logistics of separation and divorce, the co-parenting, the two of everything, the never-enough money, the figuring out how to buy the house, the external opinions, the unempathetic legal liaison, the division of the friend group, the small-town gossip, the therapy, the tears … why were these to be my experiences to bear under the watchful eyes of an eight-, six- and four-year-old?

It isn't a 'Why me?' attitude. It's 'Why wasn't I – why weren't *we* – worth not doing all that for?'

My work, now that I am emerging from a place of survival, is to tend to my fatigue by allowing my emotions to exist without judgement. I want to glow brighter and reclaim the narrative. I hope to continue to heal and grow into a woman around whom my children and relationships and dreams gather, as all of the important elements of my life circle each other in the dance of orbit. I hope to preserve positivity and energy and love to fan the spark of new love. I hope to expand and continue to hold space for other women who experience and are traumatised by betrayal.

I hope to stop counting the months. I hope to start fully living the days.

MOTHERING ON OUR OWN

ANNA SQUELCH
On choosing motherhood first

'Single mother by choice' implies that I chose to become a single mother, but I don't think anyone actually sets out to create, birth and raise a child alone. At least, I didn't. It was pure circumstance that landed me here.

My story is a common one. I left home in New Zealand and moved overseas when I was nineteen, then travelled a lot in my twenties, spending eight years living in London and Sydney.

The longest relationship I've ever been in was for two and a half years, and it ended when I was twenty-four. Since then, I've had a handful of short-lived, often chaotic relationships with men who were not great matches for me. Plus I am a double Aquarius, and I favour hyper-independence and emotional distance. As much as I always wanted to find a partner and settle down, I have always been very happy in my own company. And I guess I was just naive in thinking that *of course* it would happen eventually.

But never in my wildest dreams did I think I'd be alone and childless at thirty. As each birthday passed, I still hadn't met someone, even though I'd clocked up probably close to a hundred dates through dating apps over the course of ten years.

So, at thirty-six, I decided to freeze my eggs, in an effort to buy more time until I found the guy I'd have babies with. At the same time, I went on the sperm donor waiting list, which, at the time, was two and a half years long in New Zealand, where I live. I was wildly confident that I was just doing this to get my mum off my case, and that I'd *for sure* meet my soulmate soon enough ...

Nope.

Fast-forward to the end of 2022 and I finally received a list of donor profiles from the fertility clinic, with a deadline of four days in which to select my donor. A guy who I had dated briefly prior to the Covid-19 pandemic, and who was now a good friend, had expressed interest in being my donor some months prior, and offered again when I shared the news of my donor options with him. This time I took it more seriously, and we started to have deeper conversations about what that would look like. What would his involvement be? What wouldn't he be involved in? How would we navigate co-parenting and new relationships? Would we get a legal agreement drawn up?

Around the same time, I decided to close down the life-coaching business I had spent six years building and return to the corporate world. I'd become increasingly jaded by the personal development industry, which had been ambushed by unqualified, shady coaches during the pandemic when many lost their jobs and turned to online income, and I wanted greater financial security if I was to be bringing a child into the world.

So, at the start of 2023, I got a job offer, which meant trying to conceive would be put on hold for at least six months while I settled into my new role. I also found out during those months that I had endometriosis, despite never having had any symptoms, and I had laparoscopic surgery in July. Within five weeks of that surgery I was pregnant – the first and only time I have ever been pregnant, and likely will be.

My son, Rafferty, was born in May 2024 and completely changed my life. His father and I have a great friendship; he is an active part of Raffy's life and it's been wonderful seeing their bond grow, and having that extra set of hands to help out too. Although I hope to meet someone one day, I also feel really complete with my son and my dog, Billie. I hope when I do meet him I'm a lot more discerning than I have been in the past.

Being a single mum right from the beginning has been incredibly challenging, but I'm sure every new mum, whether partnered or not, struggles in those early months. Plus I don't know any other way. This is my normal. In the middle of the night when you're up feeding at all hours, there's no one to burp and change the baby, or bring you a cup of tea at 6 am, or cook you dinner, or take the baby off you so you can shower or have a moment to yourself. It's just you. And you are your baby's whole world. No matter how sleep-deprived you are, you just have to keep showing up.

The upside of that is that I have been able to be autonomous in my decisions as to how I parent Raffy. There's no six-week deadline looming of when my partner is going to expect me to have sex again, even when I'm completely touched out from caring for a baby 24/7. The bond my son and I have is incredibly strong. And I get to be entirely devoted to and present with my son in these crucial first years when he needs me the most.

My friends wrapped around me in a way I wasn't expecting. One of my best friends, Kiri, was in hospital with me while I laboured, and slept on the floor on a yoga mat the night Raffy was born so I wouldn't be alone. Because I'd had a C-section, once I returned home I had friends come and stay the night to help me with cooking, cleaning and holding Rafferty so I could rest. I stayed in my mum's Airbnb, which is right beneath her house, for the first six weeks after Raffy's birth. The support I've received through my Instagram followers has been incredible too – so many of them have been on this journey with me right from the start when I first started talking about having a baby via donor conception.

The sleep deprivation has been the hardest to deal with. It's really hard to think straight or make good decisions when you've had 150+ consecutive nights of broken sleep. When Raffy was a few months old, I would have friends come over and take him out for a walk in the pram so I could catch up on sleep or vacuum the house. On a few occasions I have gone to stay with my dad and stepmum, who live out of town but are happy to help me with the night feeds, take Raffy out for long pram walks and make sure I'm fed.

My biggest advice to anyone who is on a similar path is get your support systems in place now. Make a list of the people in your life who you are going to be able to call on, because you will need them. Babies have a way of bringing people together. They bring out the nurturer in all of us. If you're someone who struggles to ask for help or finds it hard to receive support, work on that, because you're going to need all the help you can get. The saying is true: it takes a village, and I'm so grateful for mine.

CARLI POPPLEWELL
On embracing new realities

I had a script. A fantasy, a dream, a plan, an imagined rite of passage that I had decided on as a young girl. It was absolute, and the idea of fracturing it brought with it such anxiety that I sometimes look back on it as a lofty and idealist prison. I found myself so attached to this narrative that I made decisions that prioritised the script over my own wellbeing.

Having grown up as the only child of a single mother, I was determined to restore the shape of 'nuclear family' to my story as an adult. My mum worked at the local pub; she often worked nights while I was alone. I saw her in various relationships and with deep financial struggles, and I longed for my father, who left our town not long after the dissolution of their relationship. They separated when I was one and I have no memories of my family being nuclear.

Life was beautiful but it was hard. I saw and experienced things that forced me to grow up earlier than I would like for my own children. So, when I found myself in the position of either choosing to become a single mother or staying in an unhealthy relationship, I struggled with that weight.

Pregnancy was, for me, a mix of equal parts grief, fear and excitement. The relationship with my baby's father was an on-again, off-again kind, and facing pregnancy alone was a challenge that I really battled with. The financial worry was overwhelming. The lack of physical and emotional support from my partner, coupled with my fear of history repeating itself, sat heavy on my heart. Pregnancy is such a vulnerable time for any woman in any circumstances; despite how unstable my relationship was, I felt an obligation to my son and myself to try and make it work. I carried a bone-deep shame that stopped me from seeking out community, instead isolating myself in a dysfunctional relationship that left me with little self-worth or self-belief.

Fast-forward a year or so after I gave birth to my son, Odin, and I was still clutching the hope that we could make a nuclear family work. In a hasty and lofty decision, we moved from Australia to New York to pursue work opportunities with the hope that this big change would be the magic we needed to restore, rebuild and redefine our family unit. I was barely living with Odin's father at the time; the on-again, off-again nature of the relationship had continued. The idea of a new and exciting city was a romantic notion that drew us all together for a period of time, but it didn't take long for the fractures to resurface.

After another year of clinging to this relationship like a life raft, I knew I had to leave. I had to relinquish my premeditated narrative and lean into trusting a new kind of journey. I needed to reach that tipping point to see that the best thing for all of us was for the relationship to end.

We had more than one therapist quit on us and later contact me to offer advice or try to shake the fear of leaving out of me, but it wasn't until I stepped back into my career that I could truly see that as an option. I was rebuilding myself as a woman and learning how to be a mother away from the support and comfort of home, and when I had a small income it gave me a pathway. Odin's father was not overly supportive of me resuming work and while I was barely making enough money to pay for daycare and monthly expenses, having an income was the first of many important steps towards independence.

Having little support returning to work and leaving Odin at a foreign daycare loaded the decision with a kind of guilt I think only a parent can understand. I would leave him early every morning as he cried and sobbed, holding out his little grabby baby hands as I ran out the door to make it to the subway on time. But, day by day, I felt myself emerging from that first-year new-mum fog and gripping the wheel.

I began to find inspiration and strength in a small group of women around me, and I built lifelong and life-saving relationships. I began to feel more connected to Odin and my motherhood than ever before and started making a plan to leave.

I put away all the money I could and, when I had enough to get a place of my own, I started looking at apartments. I visited tiny, dark New York dump after dump until one day, in Brooklyn, I opened the door to a beautiful, freshly painted, light-filled two-bedroom apartment with a quaint little kitchen and bedrooms that were actually big enough for beds. I sat in the deep-set window frame of the living room with my legs tucked underneath me and imagined us living there. I could see it so clearly that after about half an hour I called the broker, who told me if I wired US$1000 there and then, the place would be taken off the market and it would be mine.

I had to pay the broker's fee and, being foreign with no prior rental history, three months' rent upfront. That US$8500 was everything I had saved. I wired the money immediately and scrambled to find enough to get through the rest of the month. I had drained everything, but I felt lighter and richer than ever.

—

In the weeks between then and my moving date, the energy at home was stiff and fragile. We tried to use a mediator to facilitate our discussions, which quickly became problematic. The point of mediation is to have a neutral third party to help reach a point of agreement in a separation, but our mediator ended up being the third professional to weigh in and tell me to leave. I was already leaving but had hoped to do so on agreeable terms and wanted a clear plan in place when it came to how we managed caring for Odin. I couldn't bear the thought of time away from my son but I also knew that this was the reality, and I really wanted to be on the front foot for that.

We had a long and difficult separation that had some unique curveballs. After mediation failed, we ended up in court, with months and months of negotiations. It was 2020 and we were living in the epicentre of the pandemic. A city in a foreign country that was so expensive that buying milk felt impossible most days … how on earth was I going to pay for a lawyer? Odin's father placed a stay order on him, which meant that he couldn't leave the state of New York. It was emotional and triggering, and there were times when I wanted to take it all back and return to Odin's father. But then I would think about the kind of childhood I wanted for Odin, and the kind of mother I knew I wanted to be but couldn't in the space of that relationship. That is where I found most of my strength.

I leaned into the beautiful friendships I had grown in a way that I hadn't allowed myself to do in the past and found community rallying around me. Opening myself up and having other women not only help me through but lift me up was one of the most beautiful experiences and showed me just how important community is. If there is one piece of advice I could offer to any women in a similar position, it would be: *Don't be afraid to ask for the help you need*. I developed some friendships that I wouldn't trade for the world, and even though I felt ashamed and embarrassed, when I finally asked for help, I was met with the support I needed to get through.

I distinctly remember a moment, in midwinter around Christmas time, when I had taken Odin to the park. We had just moved to our new neighbourhood in Brooklyn. It was snowing and freezing cold. I missed home and my family, and there were now two obstacles between us: Covid restrictions and a stay order.

I didn't know how much longer I could survive on my salary or visa, and so many things were out of my control, but I watched my little boy make tracks with his cars across the freshly fallen snow, I took my last breath of fear and shame. I had an intense realisation that I had set up a whole new home for us and there we were, living this faraway foreign existence. I had rebuilt my life, made new friends, carved out a career, and started to find a new sort of resolve and resilience in myself. I was finding a way, even when I couldn't see any light. I remember the awestruck feeling as I smiled to myself and repeated the catchphrase, 'If you can make in in New York, you can make it anywhere.' I needed that good self-talk, that energy, to lay the foundations of a new era.

I would give anything to go back and show this scared and vulnerable version of myself just how much I would be capable of, how wonderful life was going to be, that this title of 'single mum' wasn't all doom and gloom and that we were going to be okay – actually, we were going to thrive.

Don't get me wrong: it is difficult too. There have been countless sleepless nights followed by days where my skin feels like it's shedding itself. There have been financial challenges and sometimes a gaping hole where a loving partner and father would be. But then I look at my son, and he gives me this purpose and strength and love that I never dreamed was possible. We get to make our own rituals and legacies, and build a framework for our own version of family. I have long let go of the idea that 'family' is a title that exclusively belongs to nuclear families, and have found happiness in the quieter moments.

I think it's important to acknowledge that the financial side of parenting is a really big weight that can disempower practical choices. I had limited access to finances in those first eighteen months after Odin was born and struggled to see a real-world way forward for us. It limited my ability to make empowered decisions, and it certainly didn't help with my mental health. When there is an imbalance of financial power in a relationship it can become a real obstacle to navigate with a baby. It was only once I had resumed my career that I could fully visualise a version of reality that I could practically take charge of. I was barely making enough money at the time, but even that small amount was enough to open a new door.

I often wonder: if I'd had the means to leave freely much earlier, would I have? Would the mental and emotional upheaval of it all have felt so heavy and impossible? It was very important for me to not carry a 'victim of circumstance' mindset into the financial space, and eventually I found ways to navigate it. It did require planning and a certain fastidiousness, accompanied by many adjustments. My story is proof that what might seem insurmountable – impossible, even – is certainly not the case. It's hard to see the future when you're struggling to make it through the day, but I promise you: if you just put one foot in front of the other and hold on to the delicious little hands of your baby, you can make your way through.

—

Eventually the stay order was lifted, and Odin and I were allowed to return home to Australia. I cannot begin to explain the weight I felt lift off me when I knew we were able to get back to our home. I had no idea where we were going to live, where or when I would find a job or how it would look, but having the support of a system that was familiar to me gave me a new feeling of security.

Motherhood has been my life's biggest challenge and its biggest gift, one that is built on resilience, love and grit. My passage through it wasn't as I'd dreamed it would be, but it has become a beacon that has allowed me to grow an incredibly close and formidable bond with my little boy – the most valuable thing of all. I am so honoured to be a part of this book. My hope is that, if you find yourself starved of hope, you can find solace in the stories shared here – or even simply know that you are not alone.

I love being a mum. It is the best thing about being me. It has been a tricky road to navigate. There has been a lot to relinquish but also a lot to gain. It has been lonely and isolating at times, but in those spaces I have been lucky to build a wonderful community of friends and women who have become family to me.

A big part of my therapy through this journey has been writing letters to Odin. It has been four years since my separation from his father, and in the early days those letters would help me get through my weekends without Odin. Reading back through them on harder days and looking at my life now, I realise just how lucky I am to have the beautiful joy of living in a sweet little duo.

I wonder …

I wonder if you will remember that we often ate dinner and dessert in the wrong order. That we tried hard to make our home a shouting-free zone and it always smelt like lavender. That we had way too many plants but somehow never killed any.

I wonder if you will remember our year without a car. How we walked everywhere and met all sorts of wonderful people, including Ken, our now dear friend who, although he is semi-homeless, always has a way of making us feel right at home.

I wonder if you will remember that every morning in winter there was a fire going when you woke up. That our bathroom was bright green, and cold and rickety, but our apartment felt like a warm hug.

I wonder if you will remember me saying sorry and giving you a hundred kisses because you were, once again, the last kid to be picked up from daycare. How my heart would break to see you playing cars by yourself, and how you'd spy me through the glass portal of your classroom door and your arms would immediately go into aeroplane as you raced towards me for that first delicious hug. I swear if I didn't open the door fast enough you might have smashed right into it.

I wonder if you will remember 'cool breeze, tight squeeze' as I'd blow into your ear and you'd beg for ten more tight squeezes.

I wonder if you will remember our dance parties. How you loved to make fresh juice but never drank it – you much preferred the nasty box kind, but I didn't mind. The jellybean jar was always full, even if there were only white ones left (our least favourite and by far the worst of all jellybean flavours).

I wonder if you will remember that you slept in my bed more often than not, how you loved to put your legs inside my legs and how we often slept to music.

I wonder if you will remember growing up in New York, where your favourite places (in no particular order) were the TWA Hotel, the Children's Museum, Prospect Park and, of course, the Empire State Building. It's no surprise you want to be in a band, an architect and a racing-car driver.

How wonderful it is to do life with you, my little-big love.

MELISSA MAI
On reconnecting with your heart

It's hard to fit what 'mothering on my own' is like in a single chapter of a book. I contemplate which facet of my journey most needs to be put into words, and which part single mothers most need to hear.

I've decided it doesn't matter much how I became a solo mother. What's more important is sharing the most honest version of my experience with you. Because there was nothing much that helped me during those frighteningly dark months and years of my life except knowing there was another woman out there who felt what I was feeling, who had in fact survived, and who was experiencing brighter days.

My daughter, Grace, was born in 2020, in Melbourne. It was the middle of the Covid pandemic and we were contained in one of the most locked-down cities in the world. Every single day (bar none) of the first six months after Grace's birth, I had this overwhelming feeling I was going to die. Not in the common dramatic way we use this phrase, but in the most literal way. *I felt I was going to die.* My partner at the time left me and my daughter when she was two months old to head back to his home of Los Angeles. He was going to visit his son from a previous marriage. Although he intended to return, we were in the middle of a pandemic and we knew very well there was no guarantee.

To summarise the heartbreaking journey, he didn't return for two years. And we were no longer together when he eventually did.

There were layers of pain I didn't have time to process or feel because I was in survival mode, alone and caring for a newborn as a brand-new mum. There were deep feelings of abandonment at being left at the most vulnerable time of my life, with a baby who was unwell. Feelings of anger, grief and sadness just simmered inside of me with nowhere to go.

My whole life had changed in what felt like an instant. I became a mother, I was without my partner, I was unable to work in the yoga industry the way I had. Everywhere I looked, life felt uncertain. My anxiety was crippling. I look back at those early days and they are just a blur. It's difficult for me to remember any moments of joy. The moments I remember are those of hardship and fear.

In the dark of one night, when Grace was one, I saw that the part of me that needed healing more than anything else was my nervous system. I knew there was going to be no way out of this darkness until I tended to that. The next day I made a decision to move to the Northern Rivers of New South Wales, a place I knew well. I knew I needed to be immersed in nature and a warm climate, and away from the heavy energy of fear and separateness that was still present in Melbourne. And so I did.

There was nothing logical about moving interstate, away from family. But everything inside my body was telling me that I must go. Something inside me knew that this was the wisest next step for my healing. It seemed crazy, but I followed my heart. And that, right there, is how I saved myself. Not just because the land and community gave me everything I hoped for and more. But because I started listening to and honouring my heart again. I had lost my connection to my intuition since Grace's birth. My fear and anxiety were so overwhelming, and there were many times I listened to others' advice over my own heart. And, to be fair, I was asking for a lot of advice, because I was so disconnected from my own heart.

Slowly but surely, Grace and I started finding our way. I began to trust myself again. We spent an enormous amount of time in nature. We started forming new friendships. My panic attacks got less and less frequent, and then they disappeared. My heart opened back up to life and to possibility. And, of course, I am still unfurling.

Life is still 'just us'. I'm immersed in two things – my relationship with my daughter, and my wellbeing. I'm choosing to focus on how far we've come, with gratitude and trust. There was a time I dreamed of having the capacity to start cooking again, and now I do. I dreamed of a time when my body wouldn't ache all day every day, and now it doesn't. I dreamed of a time I wouldn't be afraid to close my eyes for fear of dying, and now I can sleep soundly through the night.

Today, I honour the courage it took to listen to that quiet voice inside me.

We can forget many things during this roller-coaster that is motherhood. And sometimes we forget ourselves – our magnificence, our beauty and our innate wisdom. My greatest wish for you is that you follow your heart and your intuition. Do not let anyone convince you that you don't know what's best for you and your children.

I believe you. Keep going, one hour at a time. Because one day you will start to breathe a little more freely, and you'll find small moments of joy and they'll keep increasing. The magic you see in your child will be because of your devotion and love. And it will only be you who will know the depths of where you've journeyed to be here. You'll stand tall again, in all your dignity and grace, with a heart that's wide open again, and say, 'I did it.'

MOTHERING ON OUR OWN

ANONYMOUS
On leaving domestic violence

I am a single mother navigating the complexities of parenthood with my two beautiful children: a school-aged child and a toddler. I find myself in a unique situation as a full-time social science student, four years into a six-year degree, while also managing my own business full time.

My children have two different fathers, and my first experience with single parenthood started when I was just twenty. In that relationship we faced challenges, and we ultimately agreed that we were not right for one another. The experience taught me invaluable life lessons that have shaped who I am today. Thankfully, we maintained an amicable dynamic that allowed him to have a strong relationship with our child.

However, this was not the case with my next partner. What started as a whirlwind romance quickly turned into a tumultuous relationship filled with emotional highs and devastating lows. The journey with my second partner was characterised by significant emotional manipulation, often termed 'love bombing' and 'future faking'. I fell pregnant, but it ended in a molar pregnancy – meaning that a baby had not developed. Following this loss, our relationship became increasingly violent, leading me to make the difficult decision to leave. After our separation, he forcibly kicked down my door and entered my home, prompting police to intervene and establish a protection order for my safety.

For six months, I cut off all contact. Yet my former partner reached out to me when he hit a personal low. It was during this vulnerable time that I mistakenly believed I could save him. Despite my better judgement, I ended up getting pregnant again, and we moved in together shortly afterwards. While the initial weeks were filled with hope and optimism, the violence quickly returned, dragging me back into a cycle of abuse that I had desperately sought to escape.

Despite having what appeared to be an ideal life, complete with a home, children, a car and a business, I felt isolated and confined. My professional work transitioned to working from home due to my partner's jealousy of my interactions with others. During my second pregnancy, I faced verbal abuse and physical threats, including an attempted strangulation. I attempted to leave multiple times, only to be drawn back through promises of change.

As the violence escalated after the birth of my second child, I found myself managing everything alone. Just three days after giving birth, in my darkest moments, I sought refuge with my mother. The cycle of broken promises continued, and despite my partner's assurances that he would change, the situation only worsened. As I healed from the physical and emotional trauma, and grappled with pelvic-floor issues, I fell victim to further abuse, both sexual and physical.

I began meticulously documenting the incidents and engaged with a family lawyer to begin planning an exit strategy. However, the practicalities of leaving loomed large; finding suitable rental accommodation felt nearly impossible, especially as I worried about the stigma associated with domestic violence.

I faced security threats daily and it became paramount that I carefully orchestrate my exit without raising an alarm. After exhausting my search for rentals, and submitting more than a hundred applications, I finally received a call offering me a place. Though it wasn't available immediately, I took swift action, securing a removalist and moving myself into domestic violence crisis accommodation within just forty-eight hours. The adrenaline fuelled my determination as I packed my entire home while babywearing my then infant.

Fast-forward nearly a year, and I now manage both Family Court and criminal proceedings. Navigating the Family Court has provided a protective environment for my children, while the criminal court process has posed challenges for me as a victim of crime. Throughout this journey, I have benefited immensely from psychological support. I have come to regard domestic violence caseworkers as 'angels' for their unwavering support and guidance during these difficult times.

I firmly believe that having a support network is crucial. If it means establishing a personal village by hiring a cleaner or seeking community support, do it; self-care is pivotal. Being self-employed has provided me with the flexibility and financial autonomy to maintain my wellbeing and that of my children.

If you find yourself experiencing domestic violence, I implore you to educate yourself and seek out help. Document everything and create a well-thought-out plan for leaving. Domestic violence agencies are available to support you through this arduous process. Programs like the Escaping Violence Payment can offer critical financial assistance, helping you back on your feet. No matter how small the victories may be, prioritise self-care and embrace the joys of everyday life.

Today, I have sole care of my youngest child, with no contact from their father. Through my experiences, I've learned that sometimes 'family' is defined solely as a mother and her children. Healing is a continual journey, and I refuse to become just another statistic. Despite the adversities I faced, I have remained resilient.

It's essential to recognise that domestic violence thrives on secrecy. The perpetrators often manipulate their victims, stripping away their autonomy, and instilling self-doubt and fear. The cycle of abuse is often interspersed with moments that feel like 'good times', making it even more difficult to break away. I remain committed to advocating for awareness of domestic violence and supporting those who endure similar struggles. My story is one of resilience, hope, and the unbreakable bond between a mother and her children. It is a testament that no matter the challenges you face, you are not alone.

MOTHERING ON OUR OWN

OLA NECHYPORENKO
On the long road to peace

I am Ukrainian, from Kyiv, and I was raised in a very loving and connected family. We travelled around Europe a lot together. I grew up snowboarding, but I always wanted to try surfing – it felt so far away from where I came from. So I made the decision to travel to Sri Lanka. After two months, I came back home, sold everything I owned, finished uni and purchased a one-way ticket to Bali.

From the minute I arrived in Bali, everything felt right. It was so beautiful. I quickly got a job and started modelling, and it felt like one big amazing party.

I was at a popular venue in Bali called Deus when I first met my ex-partner. When he recounts the story, he said that the moment he saw me, he felt a strong pull and had to come straight over to me. I was on my own journey, having just arrived in Bali, and I wasn't ready to meet someone, so I kept him at a distance. But there was something about him that I felt drawn to. He was Australian, a big-wave surfer, covered in tattoos, and he seemed so free and so certain of himself. I was curious to know his character more.

It took three months of his persistence to get a date out of me and from there it was on. We had so much fun together. Our first date was at a Metallica concert, and he was friends with the band, so we were able to be on the stage with them. It was like fireworks. And for the first few years of our relationship that's what it was always like: full-on fun and travel. It felt like no one else existed for us in the whole world – it was just us two.

After a few years of what felt like a rock-star, love-fuelled relationship, we arrived home in Bali from one of our trips to Fiji and found out I was pregnant. I was twenty-three at the time and it wasn't something we'd planned but we just thought we would go for it.

During my pregnancy, my lifestyle changed dramatically. Something about growing this little life inside of me and the feeling of becoming a mum meant everything slowed down for me, yet my ex-partner kept partying and doing his own thing. We moved to Maroubra in New South Wales, and things started to shift for me. I was now in another country, and felt like I was plonked into my ex-partner's community with no community for myself.

After our son was born, like many couples, we were going through the transition of having a new baby, but my ex-partner was also working through his own personal challenges. While I was doing my best to navigate this new journey into motherhood, I also put so much of my energy into supporting him. I remember a defining moment: as I pulled to the side of a highway, with my son in the back seat of the car, and closed my eyes, I felt like I was at my breaking point.

I had been blessed to witness the beautiful partnership of my parents. They were fierce lovers and great communicators and it made me feel like I wanted to do everything I could to make it work for my son, much like my parents had done. There was still so much love there – so why not try?

—

I don't know where I got the idea of 'ten years' from, but for some reason it became this number in my head. I told myself that I was going to give this relationship everything I had, and in ten years, if nothing had changed, then I would allow myself to quit.

Things did get better. We moved back to Bali and somehow we just made our lives work together. In many ways, I feel like my ex-partner was sent for me and I was sent for him. We had an unusual lifestyle and we were both very accepting of our differences, always there to support each other. I gave him space when he needed to surf and he was always incredible at taking on more time with our son so I could work.

In January 2020, everything changed. Unlike many other countries, Bali during Covid was a great place to be. I won a place at a high-performance retreat in Uluwatu in the south of Bali, which was my first taste of my healing journey. I tapped into biohacking and spirituality; I did a lot of therapy, breathwork, hyperbaric chambers, fasting. It felt like a new starting point in my life. Every single pillar of my life was analysed, from my sleep environment to my food and every movement that I do. I was taught every little tiny thing to help elevate my life – how to meditate, and even what temperature my bedroom should be when I sleep. This retreat was really a kick-starter and unfolded a whole new world for me to discover. I wanted to learn more and more and began to unravel more about myself during the process.

My parents are among the last generation of people to have lived in the Soviet Union and it's only now that I have grown older and spent time working on my own healing journey that I recognise why they had certain beliefs and told certain stories – stories that I adopted as my own. For example, in the 90s in Ukraine, when I was born, there was a lot of crime; you were taught to be quiet and grey so you wouldn't stand out, and not to be smart or boastful because people would come and take from you. I was making good money living in Bali and I was ashamed of owning nice things and living in nice places, so I felt like I needed to hide it. I spent a lot of time unpacking this with my therapist and detaching from these stories that didn't belong to me, so I wouldn't pass these fears and stories on to my son.

—

Thursday 24 February 2022 was the day my life changed forever and everything began to unravel.

I remember it very clearly. My parents had arrived in Bali to visit us as soon as they were able to after Covid. My ex-partner and I were staying at Potato Head and I remember getting a message from my little sister, saying that full-scale Russian invasion had just started in Ukraine and they were bombing my home. I still had lots of family there, and over the coming months, the news continued to get worse and worse. Six of my family members were killed in a rocket attack while taking shelter in their house, some family members went to war and others were in hiding. These have easily been the most traumatic years of my life and, as I write this, the war is still ongoing.

Many family members had no phone reception, and I remember constantly watching the news and zooming in on images of dead people on maps and in videos, hoping that I wouldn't see my family members.

It was a strange time in my life. No one knew how to navigate it; obviously it completely consumed me and my parents, and my ex-partner wasn't sure how to support me. I'll be forever grateful for him for the first six months of the war, as he would often take our son out of the house to remove him from the constant terror and news reports streaming from my television. I couldn't seem to pull myself away from the horror. In some way it made me feel connected, as I wanted to know what was happening back home.

Those six months now feel like a blur. I didn't sleep and I honestly don't remember half of it. My father made the decision to return to Ukraine to help his parents and brother's family who managed to escape east, where things were horrific. They'd lost everything and had spent the last two months hiding, burying friends and melting snow to have some water. Because of the martial law, once Dad returned home, he wouldn't be able to leave the country again. I realised that my fifty-eight-year-old father would likely need to serve in the army and fight for our country. My parents are such a strong unit, and it didn't take long for my mum to make the decision to return home to be with my dad.

The stress of waking up every morning to check the news to see if my family was alive took its toll. At the same time, Russians were flooding into the area in Bali where I lived.

I try to live a life without anger and resentment but I admit that during this time I felt really challenged.

While my ex-partner was supportive for a long time, I think he got to a point where he didn't know how to help me and he was dismissive of what I was experiencing. He just told me to get on with it. I felt like I had to crush my emotions, withhold the tears, put on a brave face and 'move on', but how could I really 'move on'? My childhood friends were fighting, friends and family were being killed, and I felt like I couldn't process my grief and sadness at home anymore.

During this time we lived in Uluwatu and my office was in Kerobokan, an hour's drive away. For a year and a half I used that time to cry on my way to work and on the way home; it was the only time I felt safe to navigate and process sadness. Work consumed me and, as a result, my jewellery business, Olamii, flourished. I was invited to Paris and Miami for trade shows as people discovered my brand and loved it. It expanded quickly into many countries.

One area of my relationship that was solid was how my ex-partner and I supported each other's personal dreams. With twenty minutes' notice, he would take off at 4.30 in the morning to go surfing on a different island with no reception, sometimes for weeks, and I would support it, knowing how it made him happy. When he knew I had opportunities overseas, he was like, 'I've got it at home. You need to go travel.'

While we were committed to each other's lives, we were also growing apart. My ex-partner had already lived such a full and exciting life, while I felt like I was only just beginning to get started on mine. Our dreams and visions for our lives no longer matched up. Like many others, I worried if it would be possible to do it on my own. Who would want me as a single mum? I was reminded of my time with the therapist and realised those thoughts were not real; they were just stories that I needed to detach from.

Over the ten years of our relationship, in the background I was going through my residency process for Australia. My lawyer reached out and told me that if I wanted to gain citizenship, I would need to leave Bali, go to Australia and pay tax there. I told my ex-partner and made the decision to go to Australia for a month to see where I would want to base myself, and have meetings to make a foundation for Olamii. After the month, I came back to him to share my plans. I was so excited but this was not what he wanted. He was happy to spend the rest of his days surfing; I needed more. Especially knowing that all people on occupied territory of Ukraine became Russians, and I had no idea how things would unfold – I still don't.

And, just like that, I had reached the ten years that I said I would give it. We gave it a good crack and there will forever be love there, but we didn't want the same lives anymore.

—

It was incredibly hard bringing my son to Australia but my relationship with my ex-partner became unworkable and unhealthy in too many ways to move through as co-parents. The transition was harder than I expected. My son and I cried and grieved our life in Bali together.

We moved to Byron Bay, a beautiful part of Australia, which gave us access to incredible beaches where we could continue to surf. I enrolled my son into a school and the next thing I did was enrol him in a Muay Thai gym – something we both love to do and where I knew I could meet beautiful people. Bali is still a huge part of who we are: our people are there and my whole business is there, but we are finding our flow and loving life in the Bay.

It has been an incredibly challenging few years and there is no rulebook for co-parenting from two different countries. I have learned to navigate life as a solo mum and juggle the financial load of our little family. I meditate every day, go to the gym and make time for myself whenever I can. It is important for me to lead by example for my son, and even though we still work through tricky times, I know I can decide how I show up and take charge of the things in my life that I can control.

I had to start all over again. I had to be extremely disciplined to run my own company, be a single mum in a new country, and be an immigrant. I came to Australia with no community, no friends and no family, but I trusted in the process and spent a lot of time visualising the life we would create here. I believe so much in the power of manifestation, so I created this new life in my mind in fine detail: who I am, what I am doing, what I am wearing, what I am driving, who the people around me are, how I am spending my days, what I am eating, what my son is into, who our friends are, how I show up for people.

I spent so much time vividly sitting with these dreams and taking action in my life to help me get there, and I am now that woman I envisioned all those months ago. It remains a constant process in my life, and while challenges and hard days come and go, I never lose sight of those visions.

—

I am loving the process of integrating our lives in Australia. Byron is full of people of different nationalities and little communities, and my son often approaches them to ask to join their ball games. He belongs in every community. I just stand back in awe and with gratitude for the confident little human I am raising. I feel so proud of what we have created together.

We are working on building a relationship with my ex-partner's family here in Australia and that feels like a new and exciting process. It's not something I am doing for myself but for my son. I really do love and appreciate them, and while they come from such a different and unique background, I want my son to be able to embrace it all. I am hopeful that my ex-partner and I can find the way to navigate a healthy co-parenting relationship, and that he will be a big part of my son's life. I know we both have so much to give and offer our son. His dad is incredibly strong, and his mindset and belief in himself is incredible – I hope that he can continue to pass this on. Maybe one day we will have a modern blended family.

My visualisations for myself have evolved over time. Australia has slowed my life down from the intense pace of Bali. I dream of a big property in the hinterland with lots of space, a beautiful family, and a long table full of friends in my garden. I have business goals too, and it's a huge part of who I am. I have scaled my business in a way that allows me to travel more. I will return someday to Ukraine to spend some time there. I crave the simple things so much more now, like spending more time with friends. I have had such a turbulent few years that I yearn for harmony and calm waters.

Who knows, maybe 2025 is my year of peace.

AMY GRELLIN
On beautiful chaos

I have always dreamed of having a family of my own. A husband who comes home to me and our kids every night. A family that plans weekend getaways as we sit around our dining table eating dinner together, with constant chatter and beautiful chaos. A relationship that mirrors what my parents had, and still have to this day.

Never did I ever imagine I would find myself being a single mum at the age of twenty-three, pregnant with my second child and recovering from a very difficult relationship. I was a naive, terrified girl who knew she had a long, hard road ahead of her. The life that I had always envisioned and longed for had been ripped away from me. It's something I think I will always mourn.

My kids' dad had a demanding job, which moved us to Melbourne when my daughter, Carter, was three months old. I was ready for a fresh start in a new city, and I had huge hopes. This felt like the life I had always dreamed of – our own apartment, a baby and a good job that allowed me to stay at home. We were building our future together, as a family. All I wanted was to support my partner as he pursued his passion, and I did that with everything I had in me. Until it was too much.

In 2020, I fell pregnant with my son, Easton, and I couldn't imagine my life to be any more perfect. We went for family walks and drives, had breakfasts together and did lots of the 'normal' family things. Then Covid hit and my world crumbled. We were quickly moved interstate for work and things dramatically changed. I found myself trapped between keeping my family dream alive and looking out for myself, my daughter and, soon, my son. I was terrified of what my future would hold.

On Christmas night, while heavily pregnant with Easton, I packed up my car and left.

I was in survival mode for a good few months. Nothing felt real. I was in a state of shock. I was living on my own with Carter, in an unfamiliar part of Australia, and I knew I had to keep it together for her. And I was pregnant, so I tried my very best to keep my stress levels low. I had to get home to Perth and, in the thick of Covid, this proved very difficult. My world felt so small. I felt alone, like I was living in a horrible nightmare.

I remember seeing my parents and siblings waiting for me at the airport in Perth and I finally felt like I wasn't on my own. Moving back in with my parents has saved me in many ways. They have been my rock through all of this, offering the kids and me the love and stability that I couldn't provide on my own in those early days. I had nothing behind me – no money, assets or qualifications. I would be homeless without them, and I can't even begin to imagine how my life would have looked. They have allowed me to grow into the parent I have always wanted to be and am today, so I owe them everything and more.

In February 2021, I welcomed Easton into the world with my two best friends by my side. I felt so supported and safe – a vast contrast to Carter's birth – and it was the most incredible birth. I remember breaking down in labour, because I felt sad for my unborn son that his dad wouldn't be the first to meet him. But this is when I realised that my kids have the most incredible role models around them, people who would move heaven and earth for them, and that speaks louder than anything. I knew from then on that I would never allow anyone to feel sorry for my kids because of someone else's actions. I would give them everything and more, and make sure their lives were fulfilling and beautiful.

One of the hardest parts is watching Carter and Easton grow up without the father they deserve, without being able to look back on photos of their milestones and memories with him. And I'm still figuring out how to navigate those conversations and questions about why Daddy doesn't live with us, or why don't we see him often. Having to play the roles of mum and dad can be extremely tough and I sometimes can't help but hold resentment. I guess that's human nature.

However, I've learned it really does take a village. My parents have taken on much more than the grandparents' role. You will find Easton following my dad around gardening all weekend, heading to Bunnings multiple times a day or heading down to the boat for a quick fish. He is learning life skills from my dad that are shaping him, and I couldn't be more grateful because there truly is no better man.

If Easton grows up to be half of the man my dad is, I will be a very proud mum. My mum also puts a lot of her time aside, not only for the kids but for me, so that I get my 'me' time. With my parents, I don't feel alone – I feel hopeful that I can give my kids an incredible life.

Despite all of the hardship, my kids give me the strength to keep going, even when it feels like I can't and I'm failing, exhausted and overwhelmed. Every time I hear them laughing or cuddling each other, it reminds me what I'm fighting for. They deserve a life full of love, stability and happiness, and I'm determined to give that to them no matter what.

There are moments when I'm completely overwhelmed, and the exhaustion and loneliness of being a single mum hits me hard. Sometimes it's the little things, like trying to get them both bathed, fed and in bed on time. Other times, it's the bigger picture I worry about. How am I going to provide for them, protect them, or even afford a home of our own? Or it's the annoyance that someone can decide to take no responsibility, can go to work when they want, shower in peace or wake up whenever they want. But I don't want to look back on my life and feel stressed, resentful and angry – or for my kids to remember me that way. I won't allow anyone to steal more time or energy from me.

Through all the struggles, I've learned that I am stronger than I ever thought I could be. I've learned to see the beauty in the little things. I've learned to forgive myself for not being perfect. I've learned it's okay to grieve the life I once wanted too badly, and to accept and embrace change. What matters is that I show up for my kids every day and make sure they know they are so loved.

Accepting my new reality was hard. I was so scared of being a single mum – there is so much stigma attached to that. I remember begging the kids' dad to not make me a single mum. But the best thing is that my narrative is not over yet, and it's only going to keep getting better. I've grown so much as a person and found out who I really am, what lights my fire, what I'm really passionate about. The opportunities I have had are incredible, and I know I wouldn't have had them if I hadn't made the choices I made. Sometimes I find myself getting scared of who I'd be if I didn't have my kids, if I'd never experienced the trauma I did.

I truly believe that I was meant to live this life. I trust that this is my path and although it has been rough, it has taught me the most valuable lessons that are going to shape the rest of our lives. My kids would not be living as good a life as they are if none of this had happened. And for that, I'm grateful that I endured this so their lives could be better.

My life is a beautiful chaos. Not in the way I imagined it to be, but it couldn't be any more perfect.

SAMANTHA APPEL
On dreams and determination

My life is a testament to determination, resilience and the incredible strength that I drew from adversity. Today, I am a successful businesswoman and mother, with a thriving enterprise valued at $30 million. But my journey to success was far from easy. It is a story of balancing the challenges of single motherhood, rebuilding my life after heartbreak, and turning my passion for skincare into a thriving business.

I welcomed my first daughter, Gracie, into the world in February 2018. At that time, I was living in Robertson, New South Wales, with Gracie's father. Our life together revolved around truffle farming, but the relationship began to unravel. When Gracie was eight months old, her father and I separated, marking the start of a challenging new chapter in my life.

With no steady income, limited resources and the emotional weight of a separation, I found myself facing an uncertain future. Socially, I struggled explaining to people that I'd become a single mother when my daughter was only a baby. It was a vulnerable time for me and I often felt very isolated. I also had no idea how I was going to support myself and my daughter. To make matters worse, I was $50,000 in debt. However, despite the overwhelming circumstances, I remained determined to create a better life for Gracie. So, as a newly single mother, I made the difficult decision to leave Robertson and relocate to Sydney to start over with Gracie, who was only a year old at the time.

This new beginning was also an opportunity for me to finally take the leap and live out one of my greatest dreams. Driven by my own struggles with cystic acne, which had affected my self-esteem for years, I knew I wanted to help others achieve healthy skin and connect with people through the service that I provided. Skincare had always been a passion, and now it became my lifeline; I decided to start my own skincare business. But, with no money to rent a clinic or even a room, I had to think creatively.

I started by offering mobile skin treatments, going door to door with my equipment, performing facials and skin therapies in clients' homes. Before we moved to Sydney, I was taking Gracie in the car with me, driving 2.5 hours from Robertson each day, breastfeeding and juggling it all in between seeing clients. I remember multiple times having to pull over on the highway to feed her or put the dummy back in. Those were the hardest days – however, I felt so free for the first time in years, and couldn't help but think that my life was finally on the right path. Being out of a relationship that no longer serves you, or your children, is so liberating. I was so inspired to do great things.

It was an exhausting venture, however. Juggling the demands of a new business, parenting a one-year-old and struggling to pay rent left me physically and emotionally drained. Many nights, I would collapse into bed after a long day of work, only to be up early the next morning to care for Gracie and continue the hustle. The guilt of working too much and putting my daughter in full-time day care was also challenging. Yet, through it all, I never lost sight of my goal. I was determined to build something bigger – for myself and for my daughter. And even though this meant there was no balance anymore, I did what all single mothers have to do: just kept going.

Slowly but surely, my mobile skin treatments began to gain traction. Word spread about my expertise and passion for helping people achieve radiant, healthy skin. As my client base grew, so did my vision. I realised that if I could expand beyond mobile services, I could reach even more people and offer them the high-quality, personalised skincare treatments I had always envisioned.

After doing mobile services for three years, I had enough money to rent a tiny room out of a hair salon. I did this for six months, working seven days a week, but quickly outgrew the space. My first big break came when I saved enough to open my own skin clinic in Cronulla at the end of 2020. With no funding and still navigating debt, this was a monumental leap. But I had loyal clients, and their support helped me take this crucial step. I began offering advanced treatments, including skin needling and radiofrequency (RF) microneedling, which became the clinic's signature services.

Over the next few years, my business expanded rapidly. By 2024, it had grown to include ten clinics across three states. The company now employs fifty people and is valued at $30 million. My journey from mobile treatments to a multimillion-dollar enterprise is a powerful example of what can be achieved with determination, passion and hard work.

While I was building my business, I was also healing from the emotional pain of my separation. For four years, I remained focused on my career and raising Gracie, pouring all my energy into my work and family life. I believed that love was no longer on the cards for me, especially after the challenges I had faced.

However, in a 'sliding doors' moment, my life took an unexpected turn. In 2022, I met my current partner, a person who would bring love and support into my life when I least expected it. Our relationship blossomed, and together we welcomed a new addition to the family. In April 2024, I gave birth to our daughter, Theodora, marking the beginning of another beautiful chapter in my life. I feel so fortunate to have found love and grown my family after so many years of focusing on myself and my business.

Running a multimillion-dollar business while raising two young children is no easy feat, but I strive to do both with grace and determination. I have built a strong support system both at home and within my business, which allows me to balance the demands of motherhood and my entrepreneurial endeavours. I've been very fortunate to have the support of my friends, sisters and even customers along the way.

Through all the ups and downs, I remain grounded in my love for my children and my passion for skincare. I credit my success not only to hard work but also to my ability to adapt and remain resilient in the face of challenges. I truly believe that it is all a learning curve, and you need to embrace the vulnerability and flow with what the universe is giving you at that time – and wine! My story is a powerful reminder that it is possible to build a successful business, find personal fulfilment and be a devoted mother – all while navigating life's unpredictable twists and turns.

As I continue to grow my business and my family, I remain excited about the future. I am dedicated to continuing to innovate in the skincare industry, offering cutting-edge treatments that empower my clients to feel confident in their own skin. At the same time, I am committed to being a hands-on mother to Gracie and Theodora, ensuring they grow up in a loving and supportive environment.

My biggest motivation, in everything I do, is showing my girls that they are strong and independent, and I love that more and more we are seeing women as the breadwinners and not taking a back seat in their careers. If I can offer just one piece of advice to women, especially single mothers, it is to never lose vision of your personal and career goals.

I haven't studied business, and didn't know the first thing about running a business when I started. But through hard work, perseverance and a deep commitment to my vision, I have built not only a successful company but also a beautiful life for myself and my family. I truly believe when you are in fight or flight mode, and you have a passion, it will all fall into place.

LEAH PATARA
On creating safe havens

When I was twenty-seven, I felt an overwhelming sense of maternal instinct. The desire to start a family pulsed within me, a calling I had always known would come. Growing up with younger siblings had instilled confidence in my caregiving abilities, and transitioning into motherhood felt like a purpose that resonated deeply within me. I embraced my role with enthusiasm and dedication, stepping into something that felt fulfilling.

However, when I became pregnant with my first child, everything changed. I dealt with severe sickness, leaving me unable to give my partner the attention he had come to expect.

Simultaneously, my partner was concluding his professional football career, and was grappling with despair and depression as he sought to find his footing in an unfamiliar world. His emotional turmoil meant he couldn't provide the support I desperately needed during this vulnerable time. I felt immense love for my new son, but was also profoundly alone and scared as I stepped into motherhood. The thrill of new beginnings was overshadowed by uncertainty and isolation. Our relationship didn't last, and I became a solo mother for the first time.

When I met my next partner, I was eager to solidify our relationship and nurture him. For seven years we built a life together, and I invested in myself, in our relationship and in his business. Watching him interact with my son gave me hope that I had found a solid foundation for our family. Yet, as soon as I became pregnant, the dynamic shifted dramatically. Despite my sacrifices and unwavering support for his ambitions, I felt abandoned when I needed him most.

As my body transformed, my modelling career was abruptly impacted, and again I dealt with severe sickness, which left me feeling vulnerable. Despite my hope that he could support me, I found myself shouldering the emotional and aspirational weight of our relationship.

It felt like history was repeating itself.

It was September 2020 when my world truly unravelled. As the clock struck 8 pm one night, and a text from a friend jolted me from my routine. 'You're not going to believe what he posted on social media,' she wrote.

My heart sank as dread washed over me. By this time, I had blocked my partner on social media, severing ties with someone I had once considered the love of my life. Now another message chimed in, then another, until nearly thirty texts flooded my phone, each one confirming the same shocking news: he had announced our separation on social media, framing it as a 'conscious uncoupling', when that was so far from the truth.

Reading his words felt like watching a nightmare come to life. They were distorted, twisted, with every truth we'd shared reshaped to make him the hero. The man I'd built a family with was laying us bare for all to see, exposing the private corners of our lives as if they meant nothing. I was left to navigate the realities of single parenting, and I felt the crushing weight of betrayal.

The months that followed were a relentless barrage of emotional turmoil. I floated in and out of consciousness, grappling with my new reality. My former partner had left, but I was still in our home with the children. I knew I had to act; my children's safety depended on it. With determination, I packed up our lives, loaded everything onto a truck and prepared to escape to another state, seeking refuge from the chaos that had enveloped us.

But the road to safety was fraught with challenges. I was forced to navigate court proceedings while living in a cramped two-bedroom apartment I could barely afford in a chaotic environment. I found myself in a waking nightmare, abandoned by the father of my youngest two children in my forties.

Each day was a struggle for survival, and despair weighed heavily on us.

Fortunately, I reached out for help. Organisations like The Orange Door and The Salvation Army became lifelines, providing essential supplies, furniture and assistance with our bills. Their generosity allowed us to regain some stability amid the uncertainty.

Covid lockdown became a prison, and every day felt like a battle to protect my children from emotional harm. Despite the hardships, I remained resolute. I was determined to create a safe haven, no matter the cost. As I navigated this tumultuous journey, I leaned on my expertise as a doula. I understood deeply that how we birth our babies is often a reflection of how we live our lives. This knowledge became my compass, guiding me through the storm. My courage, bravery, determination and endurance emerged as I embraced my role as a mother – a sovereign mother, ready to reclaim our future. Two years later, I look back and realise how far I've come.

I now live on a dirt road in the forest, surrounded by mudbrick homes, embracing the simplicity and finding beauty in the small, wholesome moments. Surrounded by towering trees, the sound of birds and the rich earth beneath my feet, I feel grounded and whole in a way I never knew I needed. I am the primary carer of my children, savouring the true wealth of driving them to their extraordinary school each day, where they are nurtured in imagination and beauty. I teach them the values of compassion, love and resilience in my meaningful vocation.

In this new chapter, I've found true connections with people who feel like family – friends who uplift me, stand by me and bring out the best in me. I'm grounded, standing firmly on my own, proud of the woman I've become. This journey has shaped me into a strong, sovereign woman – a force to be reckoned with, unshakable in my own power.

Motherhood as a single mother was never a role I envisioned for myself – certainly not twice. The thought of navigating that journey again felt daunting, and perhaps that's why I lingered in my second relationship far longer than I should have. I was haunted by the fear of ending up alone, of facing the unknown once more. It was easier to stay than to confront the possibility of loss and disappointment.

Now, as I stand at the crossroads of my past and future, I am learning that it's okay to redefine what motherhood means to me. It's not just about the roles we play, but about the strength we find in choosing our own paths.

As I reflect on my evolution, I celebrate the strength I never knew I possessed. I rejoice in the woman I am today, and I hope my daughters will one day walk in my shoes, carrying forward the legacy of resilience and empowerment. I am determined to show them that they, too, are forces of nature. This is the reality of single parenting – a journey filled with challenges, yet rich in purpose. I am the author of my life story, and I will continue to write it on my own terms. I feel fortunate to have dodged a bullet and while life at times can be complex, my nervous system and my soul are appreciative of this humble, slow and steady life. This is just the beginning.

EVIE FARRELL
On the road less travelled

I'm sitting on a palm tree–lined white sand beach that slopes down to the aquamarine Bohol Sea, just footsteps from the fish and turtles that make their home among the corals of the Tuboc Marine Sanctuary.

I'm in the Philippines hosting a bunch of solo mums and children on a group holiday. For some, it's their first time travelling alone with their kids, and for most, it's their first time holidaying with a group. Friendships instantly formed, the kids have run off together to play and swim, and the mums have had a physical reaction: a slow release of breath, some with tears of relief and happiness.

Finally, we're on holidays with friends. We're accepted and included and the kids are having fun. We don't need to make the decisions or the plans. We're not alone.

During my fifteen years of being a solo mum to my daughter, Emmie, I've felt the range of emotions from exhausted to empowered, but the sadness of not being included in family friends' group holidays was the hardest for my heart to deal with. Not being part of a parenting twosome makes it difficult to form bestie couple connections, and while the feeling of being left out didn't bother me for myself, it broke my heart for my daughter. It's a common theme for solo mums and it always feels the worst at the times that should be the happiest, like Christmas and school holidays, when everyone is away having fun together and you're at home alone trying to entertain your kids.

So I fixed it. A few years ago, I started a passion project that has now become an actual business for me: Mumpack Trips. I host group trips for solo mums and kids (and for mums only, to escape the kids!) and I truly feel this is where I should be. It's been a long journey, but I'm almost there.

Emmie was born back in 2010, and while my heart exploded with love, shortly after, my world blew up. In retrospect, my relationship with her father hadn't been great for a long time (if ever), but I loved him so much that I had accepted very little and had lived in hope alongside growing anxiety and diminishing self-esteem. After days on end of going out and not coming home, he threw the grenade:

I don't love you, he told me, and he left.

There I was, a first-time mum, unexpectedly solo and with the sudden removal of Emmie's father came the loss of the friendship group I'd spent the most time with over the previous six years. Thank goodness for Mother's Group and the wonderful women who gathered me into their circle and their lives, and for my mum, of course – what would I have done without her?

Emmie's dad and I sold our home and I moved into a rental and went back to work earlier than planned. I had to support

Emmie and me financially and emotionally, and those first few years were mentally very, very tough. I really don't know how I got through it – and thinking about it always brings me to tears. The loneliness, the fear, the bewilderment – being abandoned at your most vulnerable is unfathomable until you realise that you don't want someone who could so heartlessly leave you as a new mum, trying to figure out how to care for a tiny baby all alone.

When I was struggling, I reminded myself that along with overwhelm comes opportunity. Opportunity to lead, to teach, to grow my daughter with the values and principles that I felt were important. To make decisions for my family based on what the two of us needed. To build a tight little family on love. And slowly, I created a stable home. But with that came the sacrifice of time together that only solo mums can understand, and working full time meant I missed a lot of the time needed to make friends with preschool mums, playgroup mums and other connections.

What was easy was making the decision to not date until Emmie was old enough to protect herself. I'd heard too many stories about the risks and the predators that target solo mums. By the time I was over her father, I didn't really care anymore. I could change a fucking light bulb myself.

While I loved being able to use the toilet alone at work, my heart was being ripped out with Emmie in long day care a few days a week (thank goodness, again, for my mum, who went part time in her job to be able to help care for Emmie). I found beautiful au pairs from Europe who lived with us and helped so much, but I wasn't with my daughter, and when she started kindergarten and was sitting at a desk surrounded by concrete while I was doing the same at my job. I knew I had to take control of our lives. I was working in the city every weekday to pay a mortgage and racing around trying to cram our life together into the weekends. I wanted time with my Emmie and I felt disconnected from her. I was missing too much.

The loss of a beautiful friend slapped me in the face and made me realise that I knew my office walls better than I did my daughter. So I hatched a plan.

We would leave Australia and travel together for a year, spending every second, minute and hour exploring the world. Emmie would grow up with a mind stretched wide by experiences and freedom and know there was always more to discover. We would be together, we would know each other. And Facebook updates from families holidaying together would no longer be my kryptonite.

I quit my job, packed up the house and rented it out, enrolled Emmie in distance education, and off we went. I used my savings, and I also started travel writing and earnt a little money along the way. We lived cheaply but we lived so well. We spent years roaming through Asia, just the two of us. It was the best life, and I'd do it all again.

I am so in awe of that brave mum who set off on an adventure to create a deeper relationship with her daughter, to share what she could and most importantly to make the memories that needed to be there, just in case. While travelling long-term like this might not be an option for everyone, carving out time with your kids and throwing responsibilities to the side, even for just a few hours, is so important.

I shared our travels on social media and solo mums began messaging me and asking how I was able to travel, and if they could join me. I'd been thinking for years about creating trips for solo mums and kids – a safe space to holiday together, where everything was organised. I ran a couple of trips in 2018 while we were still travelling, and I started them again after the pandemic. To date, I've hosted more than 300 mums and kids on my trips, and while I'm still working my corporate job, I'm hoping to be able to switch to Mumpack Trips full time very soon.

The idea of these holidays is to create precious time for mums and kids to be together with a group of new, supportive friends. I plan and run it all, so all the mums and kids have to do is relax, connect and have fun. The joy sometimes makes me cry. Mums make new friends and later visit each other and go travelling together, and their kids see that there are other children like them in solo-parent families. I usually hire an entire hotel so it's all ours and very secure. We explore and learn about culture and history and do so many fun activities, like climbing waterfalls, cooking classes and riding bikes through rice paddies. And importantly, the mums get to have a couple of cocktails without being annoyed by little tugging hands and having to be the entertainment.

It brings me so much happiness to know I've created something so positive from being a solo mum.

While becoming a solo mum was completely unexpected for me, no matter how you get here, struggles are universal. But please keep striving, keep working, know that bringing up your children on your own makes you a force that deserves the deepest respect – never let anyone make you feel less than. What you are doing is superhuman – and I see you and I think you're incredible.

Resources

Here's a comprehensive resource list for women in Australia who have left a marriage or relationship, organised by state and including national organisations. These resources cover financial support, housing, Family Court processes, family and domestic violence, and mental health support. It's advisable to reach out to these organisations directly for specific assistance tailored to individual situations.

National resources

- Women's Legal Services Australia (WLSA)
  Website: wlsa.org.au
  Provides legal advice and support for women.

- 1800RESPECT
  Phone: 1800 737 732
  Website: 1800respect.org.au
  National sexual assault, domestic and family violence counselling service.

- Lifeline
  Phone: 13 11 14
  Website: lifeline.org.au
  24/7 crisis support and suicide-prevention services.

- Beyond Blue
  Phone: 1300 22 4636
  Website: beyondblue.org.au
  Support for mental health and wellbeing.

State-by-state resources

Australian Capital Territory

- Legal Aid ACT
  Phone: 1300 654 314
  Website: legalaidact.org.au
  Offers legal assistance and information, including family law.

- Domestic Violence Crisis Service (DVCS)
  Phone: 02 6280 0900
  Website: dvcs.org.au
  Offers support and services for those experiencing domestic violence.

Queensland

- Legal Aid Queensland
  Phone: 1300 65 11 88
  Website: legalaid.qld.gov.au
  Provides legal help for family law issues.

- DVConnect
  Phone: 1800 811 811
  Website: dvconnect.org
  Offers help for those experiencing domestic, family or sexual violence.

New South Wales

- NSW Department of Communities and Justice
  Website: dcj.nsw.gov.au
  Provides information on housing and financial support.

- Legal Aid NSW
  Phone: 1300 888 529
  Website: legalaid.nsw.gov.au
  Legal assistance and information, including the Women's Domestic Violence Court Advocacy Program.

- Domestic Violence NSW
  Website: dvnsw.org.au
  Provides specialist domestic and family violence services.

RESOURCES

Northern Territory

- Legal Aid NT
  Phone: 1800 019 343
  Website: legalaid.nt.gov.au
  Help for legal issues including family law.

- Women's Safety Services of Central Australia
  Phone (24/7 crisis accommodation): 08 8952 6075
  Phone (support and outreach): 08 8953 7648
  Website: wossca.org.au
  Accommodation and support for women and children experiencing family violence.

South Australia

- Women's Community Shelters
  Website: womenscommunityshelters.org.au
  Crisis accommodation for women and children.

- Legal Services Commission South Australia
  Phone: 1300 366 424
  Website: lsc.sa.gov.au
  Offers legal assistance and information, including family law.

- Women's Safety Services SA
  Phone: 1800 800 098
  Website: womenssafetyservices.com.au
  Supports women and their children who are experiencing domestic and family violence.

Tasmania

- Tasmania Legal Aid
  Phone: 1300 366 611
  Website: legalaid.tas.gov.au
  Offers legal assistance and information, including family law.

- Women's Legal Service Tasmania
  Phone: 1800 682 468
  Website: womenslegaltas.org.au
  Community legal service in Hobart, Launceston and Burnie.

Victoria

- Victorian Legal Aid
  Phone: 1300 792 387
  Website: legalaid.vic.gov.au
  Offers legal assistance, including family law.

- Safe and Equal
  Website: safeandequal.org.au
  Provides information and resources for those experiencing family and gender-based violence.

- Safe Steps Family Violence Response Centre
  Phone: 1800 015 188
  Website: safesteps.org.au
  24/7 family violence response centre.

Western Australia

- Legal Aid Western Australia
  Phone: 1300 650 579
  Website: legalaid.wa.gov.au
  Provides help for legal issues including family law.

- Centre for Women's Safety and Wellbeing
  Website: cwsw.org.au
  Provides women's specialist domestic and family violence services, women's health and sexual assault services.

Additional resources

- Centrelink
  Website: servicesaustralia.gov.au
  For financial support and welfare services.

- Housing Connect (various states)
  Local services for housing assistance.

Acknowledgements

Firstly, to my publisher, Tahlia Anderson, who shared a connection to these stories and advocated for this book, supporting me throughout this whole process.

To copyeditor Emma Driver, project editor Lauren Carta and designer Alissa Dinallo, who all helped bring these stories to life. And to Jacinta Hardie-Grant, who initially encouraged my vision for this book.

To my family: thank you for your love and support throughout the years.

To Aunty Al: your sacrifices and steadfast presence have meant more to us than my words could ever convey. The way you've shown up for us over the years is something I will never forget.

To friends who have become like family, and to all the wonderful people in the cities we've called home who stepped in to support us: your kindness and generosity have left an indelible mark on our lives.

To my loyal dog and guardian angel, Kobe, who would sit at my feet, grounding me with her quiet assurance that I was never alone. And to Max, my boisterous puppy, who has kept me on my toes since the day we rescued him: thank you for reminding me of the joy and unpredictability of life.

To all the single and solo mums who came before us: your resilience and determination paved the way for so many others. You fought to be seen and heard, often without the support and resources we have now, and you endured the heavy weight of societal stigma with courage. We stand on your shoulders.

To the incredible women who have graciously shared their stories in this book: your openness, vulnerability and willingness to revisit challenging moments in your lives are gifts to the world. Your bravery and hope will undoubtedly inspire and uplift anyone who reads this. I am deeply honoured to have been able to share this journey with you.

Finally, to my son, Lenny: you are my greatest love and my most precious blessing. Your playfulness, sensitivity and boundless love for the world teach me every day how to live fully and joyfully. Thank you for being my heart, my anchor, and my constant source of light.

Emily-Rose Simmons @emilyrose.photographer_

Rachel Maksimovic is a proud solo mum and the host of the popular podcast *Mothering on My Own*. Rachel has been a solo mum since she was twenty weeks pregnant and is passionate about creating a community for other solo and single mothers where they feel heard, supported and less alone. She decided to share her own journey in this spirit of helping others, and the podcast hosts parenting experts and shares stories of single and solo mums on a range of topics, including finances, childcare arrangements, work–life balance, finding love again and how to build a true community.